A Bishop Speaks His Mind

EARL G. HUNT, JR.
A Bishop Speaks His Mind
A Candid View of United Methodism

Foreword by Bishop William Boyd Grove

Abingdon Press
NASHVILLE

A BISHOP SPEAKS HIS MIND

A Candid View of United Methodism

Copyright © 1987 by Abingdon Press

All rights reserved.
No part of this work may be reproduced or transmitted in any form or by any means, electronic or mechanical, including photocopying and recording, or by any information storage or retrieval system, except as may be expressly permitted by the 1976 Copyright Act or in writing from the publisher. Requests for permission should be addressed in writing to Abingdon Press, 201 Eighth Avenue, South, Nashville, TN 37202.

This book is printed on acid-free paper.

Library of Congress Cataloging-in-Publication Data

Hunt, Earl G., Jr.
  A bishop speaks his mind.
  1. United Methodist Church (U.S.) 2. Methodist Church—United States. I. Title.
BX8382.2.H86   1987   287'.6   87-1794

ISBN 0-687-03565-1
(alk. paper)

The Bible text in this publication unless otherwise indicated is from the Revised Standard Version of the Bible, copyrighted 1946, 1952, © 1971, 1973 by the Division of Christian Education of the National Council of the Churches of Christ in the U.S.A., and used by permission.

Scripture noted KJV is from the King James Version.

The excerpt on pages 39-40 from "What's Ahead for the Church?" by Albert C. Outler is used by permission of *New World Outlook*.

MANUFACTURED BY THE PARTHENON PRESS AT
NASHVILLE, TENNESSEE, UNITED STATES OF AMERICA

To
ROY HUNTER SHORT
and
JAMES SAMUEL THOMAS
Giants in the Christian community
My colleagues and treasured friends

CONTENTS

Foreword 9

Preface 13

Introduction: Establishing a Reason and
Setting for This Book 15

   1. A People Claimed by God for His Own 27

   2. Only a Layperson 48

   3. Agony and Ecstasy in a Stained-Glass Jungle 63

   4. Theology and Doxology 83

   5. On Being Heralds of God 103

   6. The "Glory of the Lighted Mind" 119

   7. Overcoming the Paralysis of Structure 137

   8. Where the Real Issues Lie 155

   9. If Morning Is to Come 176

Notes 185

FOREWORD

The United Methodist Church as a part of the body of Christ is itself a wondrous organism, an amazing interconnection of parts, each attached to the other and all working together to fulfill the purpose of the whole body.

In these recent years, however, because of pressures upon and within the body, that unity and harmony has not always been manifest. In the United States The United Methodist Church finds itself in a new and difficult situation attempting to make its witness in a culture that is increasingly secular and materialistic. We are beginning to see ourselves in a missionary stance in a society whose values are largely alien to the gospel. As a result, our church is slightly disoriented, somewhat off balance, and increasingly divided about our theology, our understanding of ministry and mission, and our Social Principles and their application. While we continue to be a strong and vibrant church supporting effective ministry all over the world, there are important questions that we must answer and significant challenges that we must address.

To this church in this society Bishop Earl G. Hunt, Jr., speaks in a book that harvests the fruit of twenty-three years of episcopal experience in our church. He attempts to "speak the truth in love" in order that "the whole body being fitted and held together by that which every joint supplies according to the proper working of each individual part causes the growth of the body for the building up of itself in love" (Eph. 4:16, paraphrase).

This book is a valuable contribution to creative dialogue within our church for a number of reasons.

First, because this is a word from a member of the Council of

Bishops. The church is looking to its bishops for strong leadership and articulate witness in these days. From those who are elected and consecrated bishops in the church much is expected. The bishops, according to the *Book of Discipline* "carry primary responsibility for ordering the life of the Church. It is their task to enable the gathered Church to worship and to evangelize faithfully" (Paragraph 501). Bishops are to "oversee the spiritual and temporal affairs of The United Methodist Church, which confesses Jesus Christ as Lord and Savior, and particularly to lead the Church in its mission of witness and service in the world" (Paragraph 514.1). The bishops are expected to be the chief pastors and teachers of the church. Because of the respect in which the office of bishop has been held historically and is held today, the bishops for the most part are trusted and their words are heeded by the church.

Second, the book's contribution is a worthy one because the particular bishop who has written the book brings rich experience and unusual personal credibility to the task. Few of our colleagues of recent times have served as active bishops for twenty-three years as has Bishop Hunt. His service in the office has spanned one of the most turbulent and dramatic periods in our nation's history: the period in which we have struggled for the soul of the nation and the civil rights movement, the war in Vietnam, the so-called sexual revolution, and the increasing secularization of our society. During this period The United Methodist Church, the most "national" of our churches, has witnessed valiantly, even heroically, to the relevance of the gospel to these social challenges. But during this same period the church has decreased in membership and today experiences the pain of conflicting opinions and confused identity.

To this church in this culture Bishop Hunt speaks his mind. He shares in this book the passion for the gospel that has made him a mighty preacher of the Word. He also shares his gift for hearing and understanding various points of view, a gift that has made him a minister of reconciliation throughout the connection.

Endowed with unusual gifts that have been developed through long experience, one who has been chosen by his

FOREWORD

colleagues to be the president of the Council of Bishops offers to us all insights that will contribute positively to the life and health of our church in our time.

> William Boyd Grove
> *Resident Bishop of the*
> *West Virginia Area*
> *The United Methodist Church*

PREFACE

United Methodism is a world church. However, this book is addressed *only* to United Methodists in the United States and attempts to deal with the condition of our church in one country.

I could write a much longer volume in praise of the multitude of good and commendable activities in which our United States church is involved and could respond vigorously to its critics. But this is not the purpose of the following chapters. Rather they are a tract for these times written from the viewpoint of a single United Methodist minister.

I am indebted to many. Professors Theodore Runyon, Walter Weaver, and Waite Willis assisted me in research. Dr. Albert C. Outler read the entire manuscript and offered constructive suggestions. Bishops W. Ralph Ward, Jr., Joel D. McDavid, James S. Thomas, Emerson Colaw, William Boyd Grove, and James Mace Ault have reviewed or discussed portions of the manuscript with me, and many revisions on my part reflect their helpfulness. I am honored by Bishop Grove's willingness to write the introduction to this volume. The Reverend Robert M. Temple, Jr., spent hours proofreading the text and also offered evaluative comments. Robert K. Feaster and H. Claude Young, Jr., were ready with prompt encouragement when my inspiration and courage failed.

I owe a debt beyond measure to my personal secretary, Nina Nailling, and our office secretary, Barbara Koehl, for typing and retyping this document. My wife, as always, allowed me to give priority to this task at the expense of time we might have spent together.

One concern is of great importance to me. My colleagues in the episcopacy and other friends among church leaders will disagree with some of the things I say in these pages. It must be understood that my positions and opinions are my own and are not intended to reflect those of the Council of Bishops or any other group or individual.

I send this book forth with an earnest prayer that its message may prove helpful in a critical hour to the church I have loved and served for forty-five years.

Earl G. Hunt, Jr.
Epiphany 1987

INTRODUCTION
Establishing a Reason and Setting for This Book

The scene was in the lobby of the Intercontinental Hotel in Nairobi, Kenya, on a Saturday night in late July, 1986. It was about 9:00 P.M. and the delegates to the Fifteenth World Methodist Conference had just returned from a special "Africa Night" program at the University of Nairobi. Anglican Bishop (now Archbishop) Desmond Tutu of South Africa was standing in the lobby with Spurgeon Dunnam, editor of the *United Methodist Reporter* and his special friend and escort. We were all in casual clothes because of the evening's informal festivities. I had not met Bishop Tutu, so I walked over to shake hands as Dunnam introduced us. "I belong to your fan club, sir," I said to the bishop and Nobel laureate who was scheduled to deliver a major address before the Conference on the following Monday and had come early to share fellowship with the Methodists. This small, remarkable man with his unfailing charm and friendliness smiled and then laughed as he took my hand and put his arm around my shoulder. "Then I should say that you are in a very precarious position, my brother," he replied, his eyes twinkling with good humor. A friend was standing nearby and snapped our picture while we both were still laughing—a picture I shall always prize greatly.

It was an unspectacular incident, but one meriting reflection. Desmond Tutu, distinguished churchman and consummately brave human being, singularly without bitterness, is daily struggling to remove the cancer of apartheid from the life of the country he loves. In a deliberately gentle and humorous vein he was acknowledging to me that the very act of admiring him could raise questions in some minds about my judgment. I doubt that the archbishop was correct, for he has a volume of support, more than he may realize, all over the world. But the point is this: his convictions are so basic to his life and ministry that he has been willing to use, always with dignity and wisdom, the impact of his high office to create a telling witness for righteousness in the human situation. This ought always to be one of the functions of a bishop, or of any faithful Christian, if commitment has meaning.

I did not want to write this book—but I had to do it, because of the seriousness of the problems and because I am a bishop of the church with an inescapable duty to witness concerning my personal impressions about its present and future health.

I.

Let me try to say something about the book itself. The reasons I did not want to write the book are that I was fearful it would be misunderstood, that critics on both ends of the spectrum would miss the points I was trying to make, that my impelling desire to be constructive and helpful would penetrate the words, if at all, imperfectly. I knew I had to be honest, but I recognized that honesty might cause some to question my loyalty to the United Methodism I love so deeply. Yet I have been permitted to see much in my pilgrimage of ministry, especially during these last twenty-three years as a bishop, and I felt obligated to share, with the genuine modesty of realized limitations, what my impressions have been and why I think we wrestle with some of the problems that torment us today. As I moved farther into the writing of these pages, it became steadily clearer to me, to my growing shame, that many times I must have contributed to the deepening of these problems rather than helping to discover their solutions.

The years of my episcopacy have covered a turbulent era in the life of the United States and the Christian community. Vietnam, the assassinations of Martin Luther King, Jr., and Robert F. Kennedy, the slow agony of our emerging conscience on civil and human rights, Watergate, the American hostages in Iran, the impact of the sexual revolution, the intrusion of psychedelic drugs into our cities and homes, epidemics of

Introduction

hijacking and terrorism, the horror of AIDS and Alzheimer's disease, the steadily growing nuclear arsenals, environmental hazards such as polluted water supplies, toxic waste dumps, Chernobyl, and arms to Iran and dollars to the Contras have unfolded alongside the frighteningly complex problems of behaviorism, sociobiology, and the new astronomy with its ongoing search for extraterrestrial intelligence. What an incredible sequence of eruptions in human history! Robert M. Hutchins said to his students at the University of Chicago: "Get ready for anything, because anything is what's going to happen!" Harking back to one of the strong influences of my own boyhood, I have thought again and again how easy it would be for a Christian to become apocalyptic in such a time, particularly if he or she is unwilling to engage in costly analytical thought and a vigorous study of the entire sweep of the Scriptures! As a matter of fact, many do become apocalyptic.

I believe in The United Methodist Church. In my own lifetime, it has striven *to be the church* in the midst of an alien society and culture, something which can prove extravagantly expensive in popularity and statistics. Our courageous Christian positions on race, women's rights, economic justice, and the elimination of the nuclear threat have caused many to misunderstand and some to leave the church. I fear that those of us who are leaders often have been to blame for these negative responses, perhaps because we are good theoretical but poor practical psychologists. However, when the history of Christianity in the latter half of the twentieth century is written, our great denomination will be recorded, I am confident, among those that were faithful in a dangerous era of human evolution.

But I must acknowledge to myself that something is deeply wrong within United Methodism and, for that matter, within all of mainstream Protestantism. This is partly the reason newer and less structured religious bodies are growing so rapidly in a day of religious hunger and spiritual wistfulness. It may be God's will for them to grow, but I cannot believe it is God's will for us *not* to grow and am convinced that the slow erosion of strength in our historic Christian denominations is bad for the soul of America. We have a more solid, more biblical, and more spiritually authentic legacy to share with the people of this nation and the world than the dazzling drama of some of the newer movements and churches, but we are hiding our lights under bushels of structure, procedure, persistent prejudice in favor of outmoded viewpoints, and a kind of theological dialogue that more often confuses than converts. Pursuit of trivia is not simply a game people play in our time; it is a tragic obsession that has found its way into the bloodstream of historic Christendom.

William H. Willimon, minister to the University and professor at Duke Divinity School, stated in an address in September 1986 that conservative churches are flourishing in this country because "they succeed at the basic intellectual task of religion, which is to provide meaning in life." He went on to say that United Methodist clergy "are not listening to what people are saying. If you don't listen, they leave."[1]

We have had to withstand the onslaughts of critics in popular periodicals and network television, as well as in the editorial pages and syndicated columns of newspapers. Perhaps they have been right in some of their indictments, but too often our humanness has kept us from acknowledging this and learning through these confrontations. Sometimes, in the responses we have made, we have chosen to criticize our critics rather than to face the issues and answer the charges raised by them—a strategy that has weakened our case in the public view and left the original problems unsolved.

During the years of my leadership in our denomination, I have discovered my human pride reacting in resentment when told we have erred as a church. In my better moments of religious insight I realize that such a reaction always interferes with genuine spiritual growth. In my desire to defend the institution in which I believe, I have sometimes found that the objectivity of my vision has been distorted by some impulsive reflex within my nature that has caused me to defend my ecclesiastical household without really bothering to examine what people say is wrong with it.

This is why I had to write this book. I believe United Methodism can set its house in order and move in the direction

INTRODUCTION

of a greater devotion to the gospel of Jesus Christ than it has ever had in the past. Also it is possible for committed clergy and laity to labor together until the kind of United Methodism of which both have dreamed is achieved. This is needed sorely for the ecumenical church and the world of our day. The problems that need to be solved and the changes that must be made are small in comparison to the task with which we have been entrusted and the claims of our divine Lord upon us as his disciples. It is time for us to realize afresh that no movement or institution can enter effectively into its tomorrows if it loses its capacity to criticize itself!

I have tried not to dodge difficult problems, but have sought rather to confront them with my own perspectives. Among those issues that I undertake to address with candor are the following:

- Caucus and quota systems
- The ecumenical movement
- Ethnic churches and our denomination
- Charismatics in United Methodism
- A simpler life-style for church leaders and members
- The plight of the small membership church
- The dangerous "aging" of our denomination
- Fear that we are drifting toward socialism
- Apprehensions about liberation theology
- Our church and the sexual revolution
- Achieving a high doctrine of the Bible
- Hunger for doctrine
- The problems of ministry today
- The need for a strong pulpit
- The future of the church-related college
- The current controversy over our philosophy of mission
- The Good News Movement
- The role of our general boards and agencies
- Sexist language
- The feminist movement
- Lingering racism and sexism in United Methodism
- The bishops' pastoral letter on the nuclear threat
- The Christian home

- The revival of the Sunday school
- The crisis of thought invoked by the new physics and technology
- Church growth
- World hunger
- The future of United Methodism: our willingness to be self-critical, to address our problems with tough love, to renew our own commitment to Wesleyan principles
- Preachers who drink

Understandably these are issues upon which a church with large and diverse membership is divided in its thinking. About some of them the General Conference has spoken. I have undertaken to address them as one bishop of the church sees them. It is my conviction that the problems confronting United Methodism will never be solved unless they are confronted by totally honest self-criticism. This is the belief that has compelled me to write these pages.

When I try to write, I prefer to deal with the kind of subject matter that is in an earlier book about my faith.[2] But this one had to be written to ease my conscience, and I send it forth with a prayer that the Holy Spirit may use it, in spite of its imperfections, to move United Methodism closer to our heavenly Father's will in a dangerous day. I devoutly pray that the candor of these chapters will not dim the reality of my devotion to my church.

II.

Let me write about being a bishop. When I retire in the summer of 1988, I shall have been a bishop for *twenty-four* years. I became a member of the Council when many of its legendary figures of modern times were still attending its meetings—people such as Herbert Welch, Matthew Clair, Jr., Ivan Lee Holt, W. Angie Smith, Willis J. King, Paul E. Martin, Ferdinand Sigg, Costen J. Harrell, Friedrich Wunderlich, Arthur J. Moore, Fred Pierce Corson, and James H. Straughn. Those early years were the twilight of the old-fashioned episcopacy in our church. We were moving into an era when the

INTRODUCTION

persistent controversy about life tenure for jurisdictional bishops, certainly not a new issue, was to reappear, complicated by the question of episcopal power in a day of strident anti-authoritarianism. A new breed of bishops began to move onto the scene, and a democratic *modus operandi* became the order of the day—something which I applauded then and applaud still. Because of this change of approach, the adjustments to a new church structure following the dissolution of the old Central Jurisdiction and the unification of The Methodist Church and the Evangelical United Brethren Church in 1968 were more complex and may have caused the episcopacy to begin a search for a new identity in the leadership of United Methodism. If so, I believe that this search has now reached a maturity which promises fresh and forceful spiritual and temporal initiatives—the kind of leadership not only mandated by our church's constitution but, I am convinced, desired by our people.

It is difficult to describe the almost inordinate affection and esteem in which I hold the distinguished men and women who are my colleagues in the Council of Bishops—a feeling certainly not unique with me in that collegial and close body. All of them are my dear and treasured friends. Because of the diversity that exists within Methodism, there are often sharp differences of conviction and opinion among us. This we accept and understand as we remain sisters and brothers in Jesus Christ.

Though important members of the Council of Bishops will disagree with some positions I have taken in this book, I shall respect and honor them in their disagreement. It is important for this to be in the record: I have written these chapters as a single individual and as one member of the Council of Bishops. What is said in no way represents the viewpoints of the Council of Bishops or any other member of it. The responsibility for the perspectives offered in this book is mine and mine alone. I shall go on loving and respecting those who view current issues and problems in vastly different ways from my own outlook, and I confidently believe that they will have the same attitude toward me. This is the essential genius and glory of the Council of Bishops, a company of strong-minded ministers of Jesus Christ chosen by The United Methodist Church for a particular and demanding task.

My own appreciation for bishops began quite early in my life. I grew up, as did my wife, in the old Methodist Episcopal Church in Johnson City, Tennessee, at that time a part of the Chattanooga Area. The first bishops I heard speak were Wilbur P. Thirkield and Charles Edward Locke.

I recall vividly an early contact with Bishop Wallace E. Brown who came to preach for several days in our home church. I was a sadly confused college freshman, struggling toward emancipation from an ultra-fundamentalistic Methodist background. One morning, by appointment, I met him in the lobby of the John Sevier Hotel in Johnson City. Because I had heard ugly rumors about the apostasy of Methodism (this was fifty years ago!), and because I had the brutal candor and innocent rudeness of youth, I asked him a very direct and blunt question, "Could a bishop of our church bring anybody to the Lord Jesus Christ?"

Someday, when I see him in heaven, I expect to thank Bishop Brown for the gentle empathy and quiet courtesy with which he replied: "My dear young friend, I saw Bishop Edwin Hughes kneeling to pray with an inquirer at the close of a preaching service not a year ago, and I myself had the privilege of presenting the gospel to the taxi driver who brought me from my train to this hotel three days ago." He could have turned aside so easily from an impulsive and nearly belligerent youth! *But he didn't.*

In those days I was an inveterate hero worshiper (sometimes I still am today); one of my heroes was Bishop Edwin Holt Hughes. While I was in university, I wrote Bishop Hughes, asking him for an autographed photograph for my dormitory room; I enclosed a personal check made out in his name, properly signed, with the amount of payment to be filled in by him. A few days later I received the handsome signed likeness which stands in my Lakeland office today, together with my check, filled in by Bishop Hughes in the amount of $1,000,000, and marked on the back in his hand "Not Sufficient Funds." Accompanying these items was a four-line doggerel composed by the inimitable bishop.

INTRODUCTION

> Whoopla, whoopla, whooplaree!
> No million bucks in Tennessee—
> So since the sum I cannot see,
> I return the check to dear Earl G.!

Later, when Mary Ann and I were married, we set up housekeeping in the garage apartment behind the home of Bishop and Mrs. Moore in Atlanta. They became treasured friends and Bishop Moore gave me my first appointment as an Accepted Supply Pastor (to use the old terminology) in a small suburban church in Atlanta.

Earlier I heard Bishop Moore preach in the Candler Chapel at Emory University and wrote Mary Ann my impressions. They were deeply sincere although perhaps romantically immature. I quote a few sentences in reminiscence:

> I have just experienced Bishop Arthur J. Moore in Chapel—something utterly unforgettable. My first glimpse of him was as he came up the walk toward Theology Building from his office on another part of the campus. I knew it was he, although I had never seen him before in my life. He was walking like a king—stately, determined, with sure and swift step. He spoke to every fellow he passed on his way in, but never hesitated a moment—I suppose he has learned not to, with the schedule he carries. He walks with the most impressive "thump, thump, thump" you could imagine. It's sort of like authority in shoes, if you understand the meaning. I think he must wear leather heels, and I can assure you he knows how to put them down!
>
> I can't describe his delivery. He didn't shout; he didn't rant. But he threw every atom of Arthur Moore's personality and body and mind and soul into every single word he uttered. It went through you, you were compelled to listen. It would have been as impossible to take your eyes away from his face while he spoke as it would have been to fly out of the sanctuary. You felt as though he had been born and redeemed and made a bishop *just for that one address!* It was indescribably moving. . . . After the service I went up and spoke to him. I didn't even have a necktie on, but I somehow knew he wouldn't mind that.

Matchless understanding, warm hilarity, and spiritual majesty—these were the varied hallmarks of my own initial contacts with the episcopacy. I have always been grateful for each of them and for a thousand other experiences that have come through the Council in these latter years.

The winds of change, both gentle and brisk, are in the air, and they are prevailing winds. They are blowing upon the episcopacy as well as upon other aspects of the church and I am convinced that we shall have a better church because of them.

The church rightly expects (even demands) vigorous, inspired, and courageous leadership from its bishops. It takes very seriously the constitutional and legislative mandates for them to "plan for the general oversight and promotion of the temporal and spiritual interests of the entire church and for carrying into effect the rules, regulations, and responsibilities prescribed and enjoined by the General Conference and in accord with the provisions set forth. . . ."[3]

Episcopal leadership, constitutionally authorized and required, is never to be replaced or superseded by leadership on the part of any or all of the general agencies of the church. While the relationship between the Bishops and the great boards and councils (the duties and prerogatives of the Judicial Council are also constitutionally prescribed) should always be collegial and cooperative, the ultimate obligation to exercise general oversight and direction of The United Methodist Church, under the General Conference, has been lodged in its Episcopacy. Any program or operational practice failing to recognize this fundamental fact is subject to challenge.

All of this imposes upon the bishops heavy responsibility for the kind and quality of leadership capable of assuring fidelity to the United Methodist version of Wesleyan religion as detailed by General Conference actions and positions, and offering prophetic spiritual guidance to the church. Such awesome requirements should be in the minds of those who elect men and women to the Episcopacy and must constantly motivate and control the bishops themselves.

I wish to affirm here, from long experience and intimate exposure to the fellowship of the Council of Bishops, that my colleagues in this high office are all deeply dedicated United Methodist ministers with a strong core of historic evangelical conviction, striving constantly to understand and do the will of

INTRODUCTION

God more acceptably in this age. They are men and women of unquestionable Christian integrity, and the mistakes which they (and I) make are mistakes of the head and not of the heart.

As I have said more lengthily in another book, I have no illusions about my office. Gilbert Keith Chesterton, that great British essayist and novelist who was such a sturdy defender of the Christian tradition and whom Shaw called "a colossal genius," declared that if he had only one sermon to preach, it would be a sermon *against Pride*.[4] I should have preferred his using the term "abuse of pride" or "false pride," but I still can relate easily to his significant thesis. An undue exaltation of pride or a wrong interpretation of authority poisons the ministry of any church leader, especially that of a bishop or district superintendent. To quote Chesterton again, the "good news of original sin" and my knowledge of the frail, fragile humanness of Earl Hunt have kept me aware that anything I am able to do to serve my Lord or to strengthen his church is always something many others have been involved in as well.

This important truth was brought home to me in a startling way some years ago. A quadrennium after I had been elected bishop I was attending a Council meeting in Chicago and saw the late Georgia Harkness at one of the open sessions. For years I had read her books, listened to her speak at General Conferences, and admired her vigorous intellectual and spiritual leadership in our church; but I had never met her. At the close of the session, I made my way to the place where she was greeting friends and waited in line to introduce myself and shake hands with her. When I began to speak, she interrupted me smilingly and said, "Oh, you are Bishop Hunt!" Then she reached into her purse and pulled out a well-used little book which she opened to a list of names, many of them bishops. "I have prayed for you every day since you were elected to this office," she said. "I knew you because I made it a point to become familiar with your likeness from photographs in order that I might pray more intelligently and warmly." I was stunned with a sense of humility and deep, glad surprise. I think I realized in that moment, as on few other occasions in my life, the sheer power of Christian fellowship and its personalized adventures in intercession. It would be impossible for me to know—or for any bishop to know—how many times his or her *effective acts of ministry* have been interrelated with the faithful intercessory prayers offered by friends and colleagues. This is enough to keep us all humble—and grateful to colleagues and Almighty God!

Therefore, with words about the book itself and my association with my fellow bishops as the context from which I write, I offer the following chapters of earnest reflection upon my own experiences and the insights that have come to me from the vantage point of the high office with which the church has honored me. I do so with honesty, or they would not be worth anything to anybody, but with the profound hope that my intentional candor will neither dim nor obliterate the image of affection for the church that I have always sought to convey. My wife and I owe The United Methodist Church so much that a hundred lifetimes would never enable us to repay that debt fully.

CHAPTER ONE

A People Claimed by God for His Own

Bishop Lesslie Newbigin is a legend in his own time. This brilliant Anglican prelate who left an indelible impression upon South India now, in the eighth decade of his life, ministers faithfully to a tiny congregation in the complex inner city of Birmingham, England. I count my brief days with him when he lectured to the preachers of the Florida Annual Conference an incomparable chapter in my Christian experience. At the close of the preface to his book *The Good Shepherd,* he wrote this:

> These short talks were prepared in the midst of the normal pressures of duty, usually late in the night before the occasion. They have no claim to profundity or originality. I hope that they may help some readers to think about the *many-sided ministry of the church* in today's world, *a ministry which has—however—one centre.* That centre is at the point where we are made sharers in the Body broken and the Blood shed for the life of the world. These addresses were given in the context of the celebration of the Eucharist. I believe that that is the proper setting for Christian teaching, and I hope that this setting may help to ensure that these talks, which deal with many different aspects of the ministry, direct attention to *the one centre.*[1]

Bishop Newbigin's profound respect for the church has never deteriorated into idolatry. When one has a deep indebtedness to the household of faith, it is almost too easy for that person to invoke uncritical rhapsodies to record the feeling.

A great American preacher stood in my Morristown, Tennessee, pulpit in 1955 and said, "The only thing really wrong with the church is our human failure to understand the glory, the greatness, and the wonder of the church of Jesus Christ."[2] Understood as the idealistic, pure dream of the Savior for his church, this kind of statement has more than a modicum of truth in it. Unfortunately, the church is made up of human beings like you and me, and our failures in discipleship inevitably reflect themselves in the quality of the church's performance in our generation.

Dr. Newbigin, in all of his provocative writings, has acknowledged this quietly, all the while maintaining his ultimate faith that the church, as it draws nearer to its Lord, will one day become an instrument that God can use more fully in history.

A slender little book from the pen of Bishop Newbigin, entitled *The Other Side of 1984* and published by the World Council of Churches in Geneva (to which organization Newbigin rendered substantial service as a one-time staff member), raises probing, courageous, and disturbing questions that earnest leaders of the church ought to ponder seriously.[3]

The church all over the Western world is in trouble today. The great revivals of religion and the startling examples of church growth are now taking place in what were once mission lands. The mainline Protestant denominations in the United States appear to be moving into an almost irreversible decline as they did in England and other countries earlier. United Methodism's conspicuous loss in membership is documentation for this statement. Even the Southern Baptists, heretofore spared the misfortune of numerical recession, show foreboding signs of inner conflict which may prove the harbinger of trouble to come.

The exceptions to ecclesiastical decline in our country are, for the most part, those religious groups that were once thought of as sects rather than as denominations. The Pentecostal churches, the Assemblies of God, and to a lesser extent the Nazarene, Wesleyan, and Free Methodist groups are experiencing growth, some of it quite dramatic. An Assembly of God church in my city has just built a sanctuary seating 10,000, which is filled nearly every Sunday. It is complemented by a veritable campus of auxiliary buildings. This church operates a home for the retired, a kindergarten, elementary and secondary schools, a bookstore, an employment bureau, music and dramatic enterprises, radio and television studios, an independent missionary program staggering in its size, and one of the most constructive ministries to young marrieds and singles that I know about anywhere. The dimensions of its operation are nearly beyond the comprehension of a United Methodist bishop! Too, it is constructively collegial in its attitude toward other churches and its involvement in efforts to better the community. There are at least five scheduled services of public worship each week—maybe more.

Another phenomenon of the modern day is the electronic church, part of it positive and helpful, and part of it dangerous and detrimental. The emergence of the Moral Majority and some of its leadership has posed a severe ethical problem for thoughtful church leaders, and an actual threat to many of the established churches endeavoring to do unselfish ministry. The old cry of the theological conservative that Christians and preachers in particular should not "meddle in politics" has been silenced dramatically in recent years. It is the conservative contingent of the Christian community, more than any other, that urges upon believers the importance of invading politics, wielding political influence and power, and helping in the election of compatible candidates. This has been a life-long conviction of the more liberal churches in our country, but we have approached the matter from a different position and with different purposes.

Bishop Richard B. Wilke, friend and colleague, has dared to write one of the most courageous essays to appear in recent years.[4] When I first read it, something deep down inside me testified to its truth, but I confess to an initial, utterly human resentment that the indictment had to be put into words and seemingly leveled at me as well as at many others. Then I read it again and gained a different perspective. Someone needed to say what Bishop Wilke said, and anyone familiar with the facts would not dare deny that there are many faithful and dedicated United Methodists for whom he has become the effective spokesperson. The book has helped me and *can* help our church immeasurably.

Let me be frank to say that I do not enjoy this kind of negative thinking or speaking about the church I so deeply love. I know many faithful pastors and many committed United Methodist laypeople in the conferences I have served who are doing yeomen's service for the Lord, and whose many-faceted witness glows with inspiring authenticity. What they do never makes the secular press, and rarely even appears in religious journals (some of which seem to be devoted more to criticism of the organized church than to the positive development of its ministries).

But honesty compels me to admit that this is not the whole story and that my own beloved United Methodist Church is faltering and failing in many places. I know that Bishop Newbigin is right when he insists that the church in today's world has but one center, "the point where we are made sharers in the Body broken and the Blood shed for the life of the world." By this he means that the church is forever a spiritual entity where the drama of Christ's passion (and his resurrection) is always the theme. It is with this conviction in my mind and heart that I have undertaken to deal with certain issues.

A Word About Context

The General Council on Ministries, with the encouragement of the Council of Bishops, last quadrennium released seventeen volumes comprising the results of a comprehensive study entitled *A Research Design for United Methodism As It Enters Its Third Century*. The members of a carefully chosen churchwide panel, the primary study source for this massive project, predicted that life-styles in our country "will continue to change at a rapid pace." Specifically the panel forecast the following:

1) Increasingly more liberal sexual attitudes
2) A modest but consistent decrease in the importance of the family

3) A decline in sexism, and a movement toward equality for women
4) A placing of higher priority on "living for today" than on making long-term plans and commitments
5) A placing of more emphasis on the individual's ability to determine his/her own life-style
6) Less importance of work or occupation as a source of an individual's identity and meaning
7) Increasing diversity within society, i.e., more separateness in life-styles among persons in differing racial and ethnic minorities, age groups, and educational levels[5]

The panel was safely ambivalent in its own attitudes toward these predicted changes in life-styles, but grimly clear in its certainty that although "the church will continue to influence the formation of ethical values for Americans, that influence will be a steadily diminishing one."[6]

I would hope that we are *not* ready to accept the dismal judgment of the panel without vigorous efforts to evolve plans and actions that can prevent many of the results they foresaw. Their principal contribution should be to disabuse our minds of an earlier triumphalism and to focus our attention upon the grueling task of dealing with the *real* world as God's witnesses and servants. Again, for serious students of the church's mission in today's world, I commend the Newbigin book *The Other Side of 1984,* with its startling analysis of where we are and its bold evangelical and biblical prescription for future efforts. It is a diary of eschatological vision by a man of tremendous faith.

One cannot deal with the context within which The United Methodist Church does its work today and fail to mention two relatively new systems that are now prominent parts of our operational pattern.

As I was reminded recently by a careful student of modern United Methodism, the most significant change that has come in our church's way of doing business during my epsicopacy has been the introduction of the *caucus* system. It was devised because there were certain critical areas of Christian concern being neglected by the general church, and unquestionably it has served to intensify our understanding of the total demands of discipleship and to sharpen our practical fidelity to them. Unofficial as this system is, it has nonetheless exerted impressive influence upon the attitudes and actions of our general boards, our general, jurisdictional, and annual conferences, and the Council of Bishops. Because it is human, it has sometimes exploited the practice of lobbying by an overuse of complicated power politics. The presentation of its concerns has been expensive economically, and may have featured the objectives of smaller percentages of our membership in a manner disproportionate to the larger goals of the entire denomination. There will come a time when United Methodism will need to rethink its caucus system in the light of the democratic process to which it has always been committed. Certainly it must remember that, since caucuses are unofficial and uncontrolled, they sometimes can be dedicated to positions and programs in violation of United Methodist principles. All of this must be weighed honestly and fairly against the recorded benefits that the caucus movement has brought to United Methodism.

Another influential factor in the recent life of our church has been the *quota* system. Born of the necessity to assure that United Methodism, in its nominations and elections, would be faithful to its commitments to ethnics, women, the handicapped, and people of different age groups, it became a sentinel watching over our integrity. In this role, the quota system has placed us in its debt. But it has also brought into the life of our church a new peril; we occasionally have sacrificed *quality* of leadership and performance to *equality* of representation—potentially a dangerous compromise for a denomination struggling to discover effective strategy in a world unfriendly to spiritual values. There ought to come a time in the history of United Methodism when intentional fairness (an important religious principle) would take over, at least to some extent, and make the quota system of secondary importance to the selection of those Christan leaders best equipped to do their jobs.

Having acknowledged both the necessity and helpfulness of the caucus and quota systems in recent years, I believe strongly that the church can never justify their employment except as temporary devices invoked during a transitional period in the life of any Christian community.

Two Characteristics of United Methodism Worth Preserving

I believe we ought to celebrate our *connectionalism*. Apart from Roman Catholicism, United Methodism is quite unique in the community of Christian churches. It is easy for our church today to be victimized by an encroaching parochialism, with its persistent emphasis on the *nearby* and the *local*. Certainly the earnest desire of individual Christians and churches to do good works in their own neighborhoods is commendable. But the problem lies in the frequent elimination of a companion emphasis upon the work of Christ *elsewhere*, even around the world.

The proper lenses for the intelligent biblical Christian have always been *bifocal*—able to see at once the importance of the *far away* and the significance of the *near-at-hand*. To be aware only of the latter is to fall victim to the kind of spiritual myopia that destroys horizons and desperately cripples the influence of the greater Church to which the smaller churches belong. In a sense the problem today is a modern manifestation of the old conflict between home missions and foreign missions, the correct answer to which has always been *"both/and"* instead of *"either/or."* To put it bluntly, United Methodism is not the kind of church that can hope to survive without a vigorous realization of the importance of the *connectionalism* represented in its far-flung missional structure. Deeply and irrevocably dependent upon the preservation of this connectionalism are precious principles such as the maintenance of a free pulpit, the conservation of horizons for believers, and the conscientious obedience to New Testament mandates. It is literally impossible for individual Christians in their local churches to express fully and satisfyingly the entirety of the mission to which the Lord has called them, except as that mission can be implemented through the complex spiritual enterprises of a worldwide body. Without forgetting our devotion to our own day-care centers, half-way houses, and the exquisite complexity of all our church ministries in a given neighborhood, we need to recover our concern for our colleges and universities, mission stations, hospitals and homes, and training places for ministers, missionaries, and Christian workers beyond our towns and cities, even those on other continents.

I deplore the term "connectional askings," a uniquely unimaginative, non-scriptural, and unspiritual label! A minister needs the teaching skills of a Mark Hopkins to guide his or her people to see beyond such a pedestrian phrase to the blessed plethora of Christlike activities so effectively concealed beneath that dismal nomenclature. Why not call it, for want of something better, "giving for others"? Let us remember that a good way to measure the spiritual vigor of any local church is to ask whether or not that congregation spends as much of its budget for others as it does for itself.

Another expression of the spirit of our connectional church is its continuing involvement in the *ecumenical* movement. While it may be true that this movement has fallen upon misfortune, or at least disinterest, in recent years (perhaps because its efforts toward structural union were premature), it is an undeniable fact that the spirit of ecumenism is more alive now than ever in the hearts of Christian people and churches. Unquestionably a major milepost has been reached in the World Council of Churches' distribution of its document *Baptism, Eucharist and Ministry*. Careful critical responses to this paper will result in its further refinement and in its immense usefulness as a door into the future.

If we take seriously our Lord's prayer in John 17, we must be far more than mildly committed to Christian unity; and our immersion in denominational details must never cause us to lessen our attention to the small but important ecumenical practices and celebrations possible now among churches. Leading our own people along paths to greater unity, even at certain risks, is an educational task and privilege. Participation in the World Methodist Council's work offers an exciting opportunity for exposure to intercommunion experiences within the Wesleyan family.

The *second* characteristic of United Methodism that I regard as worthy of conservation is *the Wesleyan heritage itself.* This is our priceless and unique treasure, our best gift to fellow Christians in other communions. It is dealt with more fully elsewhere in this book. United Methodist people have always permitted appropriate latitude in their own thinking and have never placed one another in creedal straitjackets. This is surely one of our strong qualities and one which we shall always endeavor to protect. But our differences are more marginal and peripheral than central. It is the great *historic*[7] evangelical convictions, grounded in the precepts of Scripture and Mr. Wesley's own balanced and brilliant teachings, that have held us together as a denomination across two centuries and that will hold us together in the future. Pluralism can never mean that our church is a loose association of free thinkers, or that the determinative norms of our doctrine and Social Principles are allowed to become victims of an apostate period in human history.

This does not suggest that we are unwilling to change where change is justified by new facts and evidence and by the authentic demands of ministry in a different kind of world, but it does mean that we should be especially vigilant before allowing such change to happen. We are custodians of our church's understanding of the Christian faith and the unique emphases brought by John Wesley. Therefore, we have responsibility to the entire Christian community as the church moves slowly in the direction of more significant unity.

Arenas in Which United Methodism Should Be Working

Let me suggest a number of objectives that I have come to feel should challenge our efforts as United Methodists seeking to nurture a stronger, more effective church in these times.

1. *The cultivation of a simpler life-style.* I believe that the church in our time, in order to recover its essential servant role in the human family, must deliberately discard the unnecessary accouterments of affluence which have caused its critics to accuse it of mercenary objectives and luxurious self-aggran-

dizement. The church's leadership and membership, to a large extent, must be willing to change their life-styles and to impose upon themselves once more those time-honored and sacred disciplines of austerity, prayer, study, meditation and total self-giving that through the centuries have been the most precious hallmarks of Christian commitment. What I am saying is simply this: the church, beginning with people like you and me, must be willing to pay the price involved in the recovery of its authentic image in our contemporary world, if men and women are to hear again with open minds its ancient evangel and to respond to it.

No amount of altering the church's structure or machinery will eliminate the trouble in which it finds itself. The malaise is spiritual. Even when this problem is addressed adequately by the fellowship of believers, the church cannot expect to experience widespread popular acclaim for the simple reason that it must exist and serve now in a day of enveloping secularism. The times themselves are anti-Christ; and this is the foreboding context within which Christians must realize that their witness and work are to occur. Purposeful simplicity in life-style and structure need to become preeminent goals of United Methodism in its tomorrows.

2. *A witness for righteousness.* Our communities all over the earth are filled with evil influences and practices, the kind that threaten the lives of families, young people, little children, and men and women struggling to live good, often Christian, lives in spite of a multitude of alluring temptations. Nearly always there are important people in these communities, sometimes members and leaders in our churches, who have vested interests in such practices. But the duty of the church is always clear. It must make a careful determination of the facts and of the place where the line of demarcation between right and wrong lies; and having done these things, it must lift its voice in loving firmness against wrong and in behalf of what is everlastingly right.

In my own state of Florida is a relevant example of what I mean. We have been battling the issue of casino gambling for several years, but the conflict was complicated by a proposal to institute a state-supported lottery with revenues dedicated to the improvement of public education in the state. Casino gambling posed little actual threat, mainly because most of the established businesses in Florida were against it, but the matter of a state-supported lottery was an entirely different problem. Because the welfare of the public school system had been invoked in its behalf (without any assurance that revenues gained would actually go for this purpose beyond a brief initial period), many good people were confused and secular public leaders, freighted with their own political objectives, were afraid to take a stand. Thus the cause was lost. This is the kind of situation in which the voice of The United Methodist Church, based upon its own clear pronouncement in the Social Principles, must always be strong, clear, and constant.

Other community evils, now present in some measure nearly everywhere, such as pornography, the deadly temptations of the drug culture, racial and sexual discrimination, and inadequate criminal justice programs, must be confronted with unswerving integrity and intelligent courage. To be sure, both the church and the preacher will be criticized—often by their own members. But it is better for United Methodism to be criticized now than forgotten forever! And, bless God, our system of deploying ministry enables the annual conference to stand behind the United Methodist preacher who, with bold and thoughtful honesty, dares to be God's prophet in these situations.

The beautiful little church standing on the corner of Elm and Main, with its steeple piercing the heavens, a town landmark for eighty years, must always remind human beings, sinners and saints alike, that there are those present who care deeply about what God's will is, and who are willing to speak out against injustice and unrighteousness regardless of cost.

3. *We must assure the survival of the small membership church.* At times I worry more about the future of the small membership church for which I have responsibility than anything else. It is in jeopardy everywhere in United Methodism, even though we are basically a denomination composed of small membership churches. Ways must be found

to provide more careful ministerial appointments for these pulpits, to design annual conference formulas for connectional apportionments in a manner that represents compassionate fairness to struggling congregations, and most of all to bring ringing reassurance to the devoted members of these important parishes that their denominational leaders and structures care deeply about their future.

Hundreds of times across my own ministry I have recalled the little country church in Greene County, Tennessee, where I preached my first sermon after receiving my local license as a college student. It was a frame building painted white, with a little steeple and a bell. Its dark pews were straight-backed and uncomfortable. There was a pot-bellied stove in one corner and a much abused piano with a sound out of Tin Pan Alley in the other. The windows were a cheap variety of stained glass, and the hymnals had shaped notes. The choir was a group of men and women with more enthusiasm than musical talent. The congregation was made up of plain folk, most of them older, some shabbily dressed, and all bearing the visible marks of hard toil. It was summertime, and the profusion of new fans supplied by a nearby funeral home served as ready weapons against both heat and insects. I remember the pulpit Bible in particular because the page on which my text would have appeared had been torn out, and I was compelled to begin my message with an unsuccessful appeal to memory.

But I shall never forget the love and sympathy with which the people of this tiny rural church surrounded a visiting young preacher. Gratitude warmed my heart and encouraged me to continue my plans for the ministry. I had a feeling that day, and I cherish it still, that the men and women, young people and children of that little congregation were for the most part earnestly seeking God, willing to try to follow where he seemed to be leading. The great ideas of religion appeared to be concepts with which they were both familiar and friendly: salvation, prayer, brotherhood and sisterhood, faith, life everlasting.

I have preached in many churches in many different places during the long years since that faraway Sunday afternoon. However, I have never felt that my subsequent exposure to worship in cathedrals and chapels here and abroad brought me any nearer to the central reality of the Christian Church and its New Testament purposes than my experience in that little Greene County edifice. Here, in a setting of rustic loveliness was the kingdom of Christ in microcosm. These people sang their simple trust, made their offerings, tried to live their plain lives with allegiance to Christian principles, and remembered all the while—though most of them had never graduated from high school—that the people of God have responsibility reaching literally around the world.

Perhaps this early impression helped lead me into a lifelong conviction that the most important action in the Christian community often takes place in the small membership congregation. Sometimes our ideas become too complex and sophisticated for our own good. Sometimes the techniques and programs we develop are designed more for the conspicuous larger church. In our denomination especially this is self-defeating. I thank God for my own memory of that little church in Greene County and the people who wanted to encourage and help a youth trying to say a good word for Jesus Christ. It has enabled me again and again to realize what is really important!

But I would not leave the impression that my concern for the small membership church is based only upon a nostalgic recollection from the early morning of my ministry. It rests upon solid statistical facts and upon an absolute certainty that the future strength of United Methodism will be determined largely by our ability to handle this complex problem.

4. *We must make all people welcome in our services.* Albert C. Outler, writing eighteen years ago in *World Outlook,* made a very significant observation:

> I think the future of [our church] turns a good deal on what happens in the mission of the Church to the middle class. I'm increasingly impressed that the Church may with its other interests and emphases be in the process of losing its middle class constituency. We don't have them in our hip pocket. We lost the intelligentsia in the Enlightenment, we lost the workers in the industrial revolution, we lost the country to the Pentecostals and Baptists in the agricultural revolution, and

now it seems to me that the middle class is reacting to the way we have assumed they were the golden goose and whipping boy at one and the same time. . . . I'm increasingly fearful we have taken the middle class for granted and have not ministered to them pastorally in as effective and valid a way as the gospel would seem to require.[8]

United Methodism has failed in effective ministry to the laboring class, the academic community, and the world of arts and letters. Our ministry to youth has foundered in recent years, as every pastor knows, partly because ministry to youth in today's world is difficult and complex. And we may well add to our concern our failure to reach the "yuppies"—an entirely new group come lately to the contemporary scene.

All this is complicated by the presence in many of our congregations of ethnic groups—American Blacks, Asians, Hispanics, Native Americans, Haitians, and a variety of people from a wide assortment of islands. How does the church cope with such a variegated challenge? Obviously it will never be easy, and some congregations are better equipped temperamentally and educationally to manage these opportunities than others. We say we believe in a racially and culturally integrated church—and we do! But it ought to be reasonably easy for us to understand why some of the races and cultures, after trying integrated worship and finding it unsatisfactory as far as they are concerned, elect to have their own churches. If this happens in our communities, I know of no alternative except willing and helpful cooperation.

Let me speak three special words. The first has to do with our *Black congregations.* With few exceptions, they are not growing. One reason has to be our slow and sometimes reluctant implementation of open itinerancy, which means that able and aggressive young Black preachers resist membership in our annual conference because they are painfully aware of circumscribed futures. Another reason is that our effort to have an integrated connectional structure has caused us to entice some of the best Black preachers away from local churches and annual conferences into high administrative posts in our bureaucracy with promise of larger salaries and attractive prestige. Worthy as our objectives have been, we may be standing upon the threshold of a day when we shall regret these actions. The clearest and best thought is required on the part of church leadership if this critical problem is to be addressed before it is too late.

The second special word has to do with *charismatics*. I have spoken quite extensively about my own perspective on this matter in an earlier book.[9]

One day while serving that episcopal area, I was seated in my Charlotte, North Carolina, office when the telephone rang. It was my dear friend Mike Begley, Roman Catholic bishop of Charlotte. He proposed lunch and I agreed eagerly because visiting with him was always delightful. When we sat down at the table, I said, "Mike, what's on your mind?" He looked at me very seriously and replied, "Please, Earl, tell me everything you know about the charismatic movement. My churches are more deeply involved in it every day."

The charismatic renewal has swept the Christian community like a mighty tide. It has crossed denominational lines and virtually girdled the globe. It has intellectuals and plain people, parish priests and archbishops (even cardinals!), people of refined culture and those untutored socially, young and old, members of all races and many nationalities. There was a time a few years ago when its influence seemed to be abating but as I write these paragraphs most authorities would agree that this is not now so. In a thought-provoking article in *The Christian Century* four years ago, Dean Snyder, at that time Protestant campus minister at Drexel University, characterized himself as a "closet charismatic." While delineating his own concerns about the movement, he closed his article with the following paragraph:

> As I have noted, the movement may . . . turn out to be simply a flight from responsibility rather than a plumbing of the depths of the meaninglessness of our time for the sake of a new creation. I have enough faith in the wisdom and power of the Spirit over against those seeking to manipulate the charismatic movement that I have come to consider myself aligned with their excursion—a closet charismatic.[10]

In my own conference, most of the charismatic United Methodists belong to the young and middle adult age groups. It is my opinion that those of us steeped in conventional liturgy and hymnody, devoted to beautifully structured services of worship, have sadly misinterpreted the mood and the preferences of a large segment of present-day Christians. I have long felt that the conventional church helped birth the charismatic movement because of its failure to minister adequately to the needs of the people during the difficult post–World War II era. There are striking similarities and sharp differences between the pentecostal tradition in our own church and the modern charismatic expression of the Christian faith, curious to discover and puzzling to understand. There are perils such as a wrong use of the gifts of tongues and healing and an offensive Phariseeism, and in many of our churches the movement itself has proved disturbingly divisive. A large number of our ministers trained in a different tradition—and even more of our laypeople—have experienced major difficulty accepting this heady phenomenon of modern religion. I confess that I have had a struggle with some of the issues.

Nevertheless I am convinced that United Methodism needs to accept and welcome those sane and intelligent charismatic Christians who believe in our doctrine and program and who can associate themselves loyally and constructively with our congregations. It is a historical fact that our church and other mainline denominations over a long period of time neglected the person, presence, and power of the Holy Spirit. This was a point made in a telling way by Lesslie Newbigin in one of his earlier books. Some of the very finest preachers and laypeople I know in my own annual conference and elsewhere in United Methodism are of charismatic or near-charismatic persuasion. They are my friends and sometimes I have called upon them to pray for and with me concerning some matter of great concern in my wife's and my lives. They have been, for the most part, supportive of the programs I have endeavored to promote for the general church and on an annual conference level. They are literate Christians and tithers, and they are committed to a level of discipleship about which most of us speak but which we do not attain. I have known theologically *conservative* and theologically *liberal* charismatic Christians! However, all with whom I have had experience believe in and teach conversion, the experience of the New Birth, and a life of spiritual victory controlled by the realized presence of the Holy Spirit. They are diligent and careful students of the Bible, although often without the kind of background some of us have because of more formal study.

I believe that to read these good and genuinely committed people out of the fellowship of United Methodism would constitute a grave error on our part and contribute even further to the diminution of our denominational and spiritual strength. Perhaps, with our friendship and trust, they can become a significant part of the ultimate answer to our church's problems.

My third special word is about the *poor.* Every church—but especially every large and basically affluent church—needs poor people in its membership. Once, some years ago, I went to a city in my episcopal area to consecrate a costly new Gothic edifice complete with a surrounding campus of complementary buildings—elaborate housing for a distinguished and wealthy congregation. Its architecture was exquisite and its aesthetic quality breathtaking. When I entered the great stone pulpit, I literally felt overwhelmed by the grandeur of my environment. Quite impulsively I shocked myself and my hearers by exclaiming before announcing my text, "My, but you folk are going to have to find a lot of poor families to be members here, in order to justify what you've done!"

I was right. The local church that makes no effort to include some of the innumerable poor in its ecclesiastical family, helping them sense the dignity that is their birthright as children of God and honoring them as valued participants in worship and program, can hardly expect the Lord Jesus to feel at home in its fellowship. Moreover, for that church to miss opportunities to lend assistance to the less privileged in finding employment and managing family crises is for it to be guilty of prostituting the elemental principles of Christian mission and denying its own heavenly identity.

Every church needs poor people—possibly even more than they need it!

5. Another very serious problem is what Warren J. Hartman, research director of the General Board of Discipleship, has called *the "graying" or aging of United Methodist congregations*—something that appears to be taking place more quickly in our churches than in the general population of the United States. Supporting figures given by Dr. Hartman indicate that while 11.8 percent of the United States population is over 65 years of age, 21.3 percent of those attending our United Methodist services and participating in our programs are over 65, with a dramatic increase expected in the years just ahead. Hartman has pointed out further that 34.4 percent of our congregational attendants are *over 55,* with only 12.4 percent between 19 and 34 years (against 28.4 percent in the general United States population).[11]

This is one of the most critical signs confronting us. Unless a great church can continue to enlist and challenge young adults and youth, its future is uncertain. My own impressions, from reading recent literature and talking with leaders of other communions, is that the more rapidly growing denominations, those targeting in their programs specific needs of youth, young adult singles, and young families, are moving swiftly in the direction of heavier figures for these age groups—this in spite of increasing longevity where both church members and general population are concerned. In my own conference, I have noted that the so-called more evangelical and even charismatic churches boast almost a preponderance of younger members, particularly those popularly referred to as "yuppies" or neo-traditionalists. A far more conservative climate on college and university campuses and among young professionals and business people throughout our nation may help explain this fact. At any rate, United Methodism would be well warned at this moment in its history that one of its most creative and urgent opportunities lies in building programs tailored to appeal to youth and young adults and to meet specifically their contemporary needs.

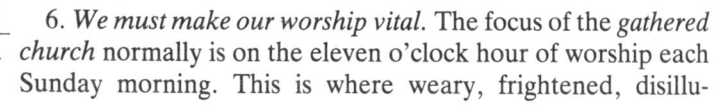

6. *We must make our worship vital.* The focus of the *gathered church* normally is on the eleven o'clock hour of worship each Sunday morning. This is where weary, frightened, disillu-

sioned, tempted men and women, often bearing heavy burdens of guilt, assemble themselves (along, of course, with others who have reason to be joyful and thankful) in search of relief, forgiveness, hope, and restoration. Ideally, behind all this is the sublimest of human impulses to ascribe praise, adoration, and gratitude to Almighty God through worship. Music, congregational hymn singing, liturgies with prayers and responses, periodic Holy Communion, and the reading and preaching of the Word are the usual ingredients of such an event. That worship is more than merely a horizontal or human transaction needs to be emphasized especially. While it is to give glory and praise to God and to allow his grace once again to enter our penitent spirits with redeeming and liberating power, we also experience the ineffable mystery that comes to the person who enters church with simple, childlike faith and surrenders fully to the strong ministries of Word and Sacrament. Teresa of Avila, the sixteenth-century Spanish mystic and saint, spoke of it in haunting words: "He has never ceased to fix His gaze upon you. Is it too much, then, to ask that you withdraw your gaze from exterior things to contemplate Him sometimes? . . . He values your glance so highly that He will neglect no means to ingratiate Himself with you."[12]

Wesley often insisted that there is an objective holiness in the Word and the Sacrament as they are proclaimed and celebrated in the church and unless this objective holiness produces a subjective holiness in the people, the church is not really the church at all. He also taught that faith itself is a gift of the Holy Spirit that enables a man or a woman to comprehend spiritual realities, the things that belong to God. It seems to me that the entire theory of corporate worship is here, for the Holy Spirit informs the message of the minister (also the anthems of the choir and the remainder of the order of service) and instructs the minds and hearts of the worshipers. This produces a redemptive interaction between chancel and pew, and so enables God to do again his wonderworks in the lives of the people. The cleansing and refreshing springs of religious power flow irresistibly through that traditional hour in God's house, and the result is restoration of vision and renewal of strength for purposeful and courageous living across a new week—living infectious with love and redemptive and daring in purpose. It is intended and expected that the Holy Spirit through worship will *transform* a human life, no matter what need is present.

It does not always happen in this way. The late Samuel Miller of Harvard put it cryptically when he described the eleven o'clock worship service as "almost supremely a place where the bankruptcy of modern ecclesiasticism is apparent."[13] One has difficulty imagining any individual receiving what Paul Tillich called an "ontological shock" in the average church service. Often its content and impact are more akin to Sören Kierkegaard's word "twaddle." The raw, naked power of a gospel so revolutionary that its transcendent force is unpredictable and uncontrollable is simply absent at the eleven o'clock hour on Sunday morning in many of our churches. The Holy Spirit is present but not regnant on these occasions, and so nothing of shattering significance takes place. Perhaps this, more than anything else, explains the problem of the modern church. Vital worship that reaches down wherever human need is and brings the healing love of God in Jesus Christ to the person with that need gives a church power and creates for it an image in the community that impels its own members and others beyond its fellowship, including those to whom religion has never had meaning, to come and see what is happening and, under God, to be saved.

Making worship vital is the *sine qua non* of any living church.

A Concluding Word

Humanly speaking, the church is fighting for its very life today. The mood of the world in this moment of time borders upon a new paganism, and it is easy for one without faith to believe that the soil in which the seed of the gospel has been sown is barren. Karl Barth reminded us years ago that the church is not only the place where men find God; it is also the place where men take their last stand against God, and some of us have glimpsed the truth of this.

But the church is of God and will be preserved to the end of time, so the ritual of The United Methodist Church says and so we affirm.[14] I do not read anywhere in Holy Writ that The United Methodist Church will endure to the end of time. This, I must remind myself as well as you, will depend on how you and I, under God, are able to manage our problems and opportunities.

CHAPTER TWO

Only a Layperson

Sometimes I find myself wondering, in spite of the commendable efforts to equalize clerical and lay representation in our conferences, if in many ways United Methodism remains essentially a "preacher-operated" church. Philosophically most of us who are ordained would either deplore or deny this statement. To do otherwise would confront us with the embarrassment of acknowledging that we must depend upon faithful and loyal laypersons to provide the economic resources for creating and sustaining the structures and programs largely conceived and designed by clergy. To be sure, in a sense such a situation is inevitable, if for no other reason than that ordained people have more time and professional training for ecclesiastical initiative than those not ordained.

This kind of imbalance in leadership aggression has been supported across many decades by the persistent and affectionate confidence that traditional laypeople have evidenced in ministers. However, for some time signs have been gathering to suggest that such confidence, often taken for granted by those of us who are clergy, may be diminishing dangerously. It is my conviction that laypeople still deeply desire to respect preachers, but that such respect is no longer conferred automatically because of habit or tradition. The time has come when it must be earned; and this, I think, is not an unfortunate development.

A painful awareness has haunted me in recent years. Elements of the ancient ministerial mystique (which traditionally has evoked lay confidence in our calling) have begun to suffer deterioration. Ministers, perhaps bishops too, have seemed to invest more thought and concern in their own economic advantages and power bases than in spiritual integrity and disciplined commitment. It is sometimes embarrassing to compute the amount of time spent in annual conference sessions in debate about minimum salaries, pension programs, and insurance plans. The percentage of an annual conference budget allocated to ministerial benefits of one kind or another is staggering. It would be difficult to insist that all of this does not constitute evidence of a growing clericalism in a church where intelligent laypeople are at least entitled to ask probing questions about their role in determining policies. It needs to be said, however, that far more than a faithful remnant of ministerial members of our annual conferences are themselves deeply agitated over such developments.

An important characteristic of our time has been the inclusion of laypeople in the ministry itself. Elton Trueblood, a famous Quaker Christian, asserts that the actual "abolition of the laity" became a viable concept during the Reformation, envisioned by Martin Luther in his teaching about the priesthood of believers.[1] Luther, however, did not make a serious effort to implement the idea. It remained for John R. Mott in his 1931 Ayer Lectures at Colgate-Rochester Divinity School, later published under the title *Liberating the Lay Forces of Christianity,* to provide imaginative impetus to the practice of lay ministry in our time.[2] It would be difficult to evaluate with sufficient enthusiasm the impact which movements and programs led by dedicated laypeople has made upon the Christian community, including United Methodism, in the last fifty years.

Basic to all of this, and of even more sweeping importance, is their role in thousands of local churches and (in United Methodism as well as many other denominations) in policymaking conclaves on higher levels. But the fact remains that multitudes of our laypeople are still poorly informed about issues related to the church and its mission, sometimes because we preachers are notoriously poor teachers. Also the general church until recently has seldom bothered to provide effective modern communication assistance. This problem is a major one demanding careful and constant attention. Many of the positions taken by our church in today's world require interpretation to our people, and failure at this point is sure to divide congregations and encourage an exodus of members.

Urging the laity to have a larger voice in church affairs may mean facing the fact that the policies and pronouncements of the church, as a result, could become more reactionary and less prophetic. By and large, the majority of laypeople are more conservative than preachers, perhaps because they have not had the same kind of education and also because they have lived less sheltered lives and have seen their idealism modified by daily reality. This is particularly true now when reaction seems the order of the hour and (at the time of this writing) the political mood of the United States is systemically rightest. The presence of women, particularly those who belong to United Methodist Women, in our modern church would lessen such a possibility because of their informed grasp of more liberal perspectives in the church's social mission. And it must be said that United Methodism today has a substantial number of courageously objective, forward-looking laypeople of *both* sexes. But, on balance, I suspect that my basic hypothesis would still hold.

A special tribute needs to be paid to United Methodist Women. They have achieved a level of participation and commitment which, in most sections of our church, borders on being miraculous. In the Florida Conference, for example, their annual budget is $839,000, raised completely and without visible difficulty. Attendance at their conference schools of Christian mission and their annual meetings is phenomenal, and the *esprit de corps* of their organization is an inspiration to behold. While their stewardship of funds is precisely focused upon their specifically approved projects, it must be remembered that most of their members contribute also, as individuals or as partners in family units, to the support of local church programs. This remarkable fellowship of dedicated women, whatever else may be said about it, sets an example of lay loyalty and involvement challenging to the entire church. Perhaps the open secret of their success is expertise in leadership development.

But, having said these things, I return to my first concern. Across the church, or at least in those episcopal areas where I have served, there is a growing manifestation of puzzled anxiety and often deliberate disapproval where many of the official positions and programs of United Methodism are concerned. My own feeling is that those of us in leadership have not acknowledged this fact adequately and have failed to take appropriate and effective steps to correct it. Too often we have gone our blissful way as clergy people, dreaming our dreams, fashioning our position papers, crafting our programs and proposing our budgets, without remembering, as we should always do, our sacred obligation to seek counsel and wisdom from responsible laypeople. We may be perilously close to the danger point where a *crisis in lay confidence* is concerned.

What Are the Average Layperson's Complaints?

My own experience in this position would lead me to believe that there are certain things that the *ordinary* layperson fears in our church today. The list would include the following:

1. While they join clergy in abhorring war and in a growing awareness of the nuclear peril, many of them fear that the church will settle for an inadequate national defense in a day of massive international danger.

2. Most of them would deplore a neo-Fascist approach to law and order, but they are enormously apprehensive about neighborhood crime and violence, sometimes wondering why the church does not appear to take a more effective role in overcoming the drug menace, pornography, sexual aberrations, and the many evil deeds that result from these community threats instead of concentrating most of its energies on larger systemic wrongs such as racism, sexism, and economic injustice. The more responsible laypeople would not wish such larger wrongs to be neglected, but would like to see a denominational focus upon the others as well. The frightening specter of *crack cocaine* among parents and teachers in Miami, for example, makes less immediate and identifiable problems, even though causally related to the drug peril, pale into insignificance.

3. They have a growing concern that a compromise of biblical teachings about human sexuality, particularly in some sections of the church, will weaken or destroy the home.

4. They wonder if the church is directing enough attention to the preservation of ancient and revered landmarks of civilization such as the Bible, governments that protect human freedoms, the institution of marriage, a sane commitment to the old-time work ethic, and the cultivation of integrity in human relationships.

5. They are afraid that the grand old words God, prayer, salvation, purity, patriotism, faith, and hope will become, in Ernest Hemingway's colorful expression in *A Farewell to Arms,* "hollow" and therefore meaningless.

6. The more thoughtful among them fear that our church will insist on superimposing the hermeneutic of Latin American liberation theology upon the situation in the United States without realizing that many of its principal motifs are not appropriate to North American experience. They are frankly afraid that our denomination is drifting rapidly in the direction of Socialism and that it has lost interest in the preservation of free enterprise and the redemption of the economic philosophy that supports it.[3]

In addition to the fears that I have detected in literally thousands of grass-roots laypeople in our church today, there are a number of practical situations which I am convinced will have diminishing tolerance from church members in the future. Let me list a few of these:

1. Lazy ministers
2. A church that overlooks moral laxity in its clergy
3. A pulpit that doesn't preach
4. Constantly growing overhead costs occasioned by visibly non-productive structures and programs
5. Doctrinal apostasy—meaning a denial, compromise, or neglect of that which many laypersons innately feel to be the essence of biblical religion. This concern is often the result of misinformation disseminated by a variety of fundamentalist or schismatic groups, but not always
6. The superimposing from above of programs and askings, usually constantly escalating, poorly explained, and clerically designed

7. Being "included out" of decision-making on levels that attract headlines and telecasts
8. A church that inaccurately assesses the needs of its members and constituents and, often unintentionally, fails to develop a warm, caring, redemptive ministry to hurting human beings
9. Failure to practice evangelism
10. Reluctance to probe for the contemporary meanings of Wesley's theology and so to search for deeper spiritual experiences

In my judgment, based on exposure to hundreds and even thousands of laypeople in the areas I have been privileged to serve, our church's unwillingness to acknowledge with honesty and address with effectiveness matters such as these is pushing us ever nearer to a breaking point in our relationship to the *average* member of The United Methodist Church. I know, of course, that there are dramatic exceptions, and some of these have already been mentioned.

I am also aware that the introduction of better educational processes in local congregations, as well as on higher administrative levels, would improve the situation vastly. Many of our current members have come to us from other denominations, or from none at all, and are innocently ignorant of the mandates of Wesleyan religion and the intentions of United Methodism in its social pronouncements and actions. The nature of our times and the general religious climate, dramatized by the secular press, talk shows, and popular television, make it necessary for us to undertake careful strategy in communication and persistent education *without compromising our basic convictions* if we intend to remain strong enough as a denomination to sustain our mission in the world.

The Other Side of the Picture

In the dismal days of the Great Depression, a strong local church was foundering on the shoals of division, apathy, and uncertainty about its mission. A faithful pastor's heart was being broken. Very quietly, a woman with two doctoral degrees, beloved professor at a local university, sought out a pre-theological student who had grown up in the church and was known by those on all sides of its current controversies. She said to him, "I have our pastor's permission to ask you to give your afternoons for six months to a program of visitation, carrying a message of love and understanding into every home of our congregation. They will listen to you because you are young and they want to encourage you and help you prepare to be a preacher. I'll pay you for this, enough money to see you through your first year of seminary. Will you do it?" The young man agreed, and then asked the professor why she proposed it. She replied, "I felt I *ought* . . . the church has meant so much to me."

The little word "ought" has been lost from the vocabularies of too many of us who call ourselves Christian. It is the verb, or rather the verb auxiliary, of discipleship. We who are clergy and laity must feel it stirring in our souls again, even now, if the church is to have meaning at the end of this century.

I have spoken at length about the church's obligation to allay certain fears harbored by laypeople, to bring relief to what are often their sincere agonies. *But there is another side of the picture.* Average laypersons, ordinary or extraordinary, have obligations because they have given their lives to Almighty God through the acceptance of Jesus Christ as Savior and Lord.

It is easy for a church member to fall into a trap of chronic negativism, to reach the point where he or she experiences a kind of unholy pleasure in criticizing either the minister or the denomination. On some occasions I have felt that my ability to bring a satisfactory response to a person's persistent accusation against his or her church has succeeded in producing not relief and joy, but displeasure and resentment. I am sure most of us have learned the sad truth that some of our critics really do not wish their charges answered properly and helpfully.

It is also easy for some laypeople to become so enamored with the blessings of religion that they overlook almost entirely its responsibilities. We are familiar with the individual who allows his or her physical appetite to produce gluttonous eating, and never bothers to work off an overload of calories in disciplined exercise. Such a man or woman becomes physically obese—often to a dangerous extent. There is such a thing as *spiritual obesity* as well. It is possible for a Christian to luxuriate in the Bible's blessings and promises until a religious exuberance captures his or her soul, and yet never express that spiritual experience in practical service to the local church or in the assumption of the obligation that is always the companion of privilege. He or she becomes a victim of *spiritual obesity,* one of the Christian community's less lovely sights.

John R. Mott, writing fifty-five years ago, made the same point:

> A multitude of laymen are to-day in serious danger. It is positively perilous for them to hear more sermons, attend more Bible classes and open forums, and read more religious ethical works, unless accompanying it all there be afforded day by day an adequate outlet for their new-found truth.[4]

It is time for us to remember the words of our Lord recorded in Luke 9:23: "And he said to them all, 'If any man would come after me, let him deny himself and take up his cross daily and follow me.' " This is a stern vocalization of the demand of Christian discipleship. Many of us, clergy and laity alike, habitually focus attention on the gospel's promises—and they are very real and precious—but regularly neglect the duties that rest on every man and woman who have received the forgiveness of Jesus Christ. To go back to the story of the professor, it is important for the average layperson in United Methodism to appropriate the deep meanings of the word "ought"—to accept faithfully the obligations that rest on him or her because of Jesus Christ's gift of salvation. If the church does deal honestly with the layperson's agonies, then the layperson must confront courageously the heavy tasks of intelligent and effective church membership.

The kind of thing that I hope can happen to the dedicated layperson, and between that person and the minister, will require careful communication and education through available forums. There are national, jurisdictional, and annual conference convocations for United Methodist men where this can occur. It might be helpful for certain elementary themes related to lay discipleship to be included in the agendas for similar meetings of United Methodist women. Too, many annual conferences have organizations of conference and district lay leaders where educational programs can be devised and implemented. With all of this in mind, let me suggest certain emphases that are basic but always relevant:

1. It is the responsibility of the average layperson in our church to become a *literate Christian.* When I was pastor in Morristown, Tennessee, many years ago, a dedicated young physician who was a member of my church attended our family and particularly my sick parents who lived with us. While he did not specialize in obstetrics, still he delivered many babies in his practice. This often involved hours of waiting in the hospital. I learned by accident that he had purchased a complete set of *The Interpreter's Bible,* quite new in those days, and was spending his time reading it from beginning to end while waiting for his patients to deliver! He had taken seriously one of the obligations of a Christian and was informing himself about the Book.

Being a literate Christian also means designing a literary diet which will give a person a *balanced* knowledge of what is happening in the Christian world. Among other things, this can mean not accepting blindly the evaluations of a secular press where the church's positions and programs are concerned, but seeking interpretations of such positions and programs in a responsible *religious* press and in books written by reverent Christian leaders.

2. The average layperson should protect the integrity of a *free pulpit* at all costs. One of the intrinsic glories of our denomination is the support with which it is able to surround a responsible minister who undertakes to preach the Word honestly and courageously, and not in response to the popular and perhaps prejudiced expectations of some members of the congregation. The free pulpit is an indispensable ingredient of democracy, important to the nation as well as to the church.

3. The average layperson committed to the Wesleyan interpretation of the Christian faith should accept the fact that Christianity has two dimensions, *vertical and horizontal.* The entire gospel always includes its social expression. It is impossible for an individual to be wholly saved until his or her brother is also saved, because, in the memorable words of John Donne, "I am involved in mankind."[5] This is what Wesley meant when he affirmed that there is no holiness apart from social holiness—often a difficult doctrine for the prejudiced man or woman to accept. One of the functions of good religion is to enable an individual to separate convictions from prejudices, and with God's help to rid himself or herself of the prejudices. The faithful minister is required to proclaim social righteousness, and the average layperson, even when he or she cannot agree immediately, has no right to silence that minister.

4. The lay member should strive meticulously to glean and evaluate *all* available facts before vocalizing judgments about issues that have to do with the local church or the denomination. This is simply elemental honesty and fairness.

5. The average layperson should seek to be a true friend to his or her pastor—a warm encourager when things are moving toward God and better days, a compassionate critic when things are off-track and the minister shares responsibility; and sometimes, if the degree of intimacy warrants it, a discreet confidant who will listen (and never tell!) when the soul's dark night has come to the minister.

6. The church member should realize always that the concept of the priesthood of believers makes him or her a minister also, though not ordained, and so causes destructive criticisms of the preacher to be, in the end, a kind of family denial. This may help produce empathy and a saving restraint when there is temptation to gossip and condemn.

7. The average layperson should give generously of his or her material means in the support of God's work, channeling much of that gift, in accordance with the membership covenant, to the church. I dare to suggest as well that such a gift should always be in proper proportion to an individual's income and resources. I believe in tithing and my wife and I have practiced it throughout our ministry; but I also believe that for some of us tithing is not enough. I remember a millionaire layperson whose bishop I was in Western North Carolina who gladly gave to the Lord and his church *nine-tenths* of his annual income, living comfortably on the tenth that remained.

The church member who has not made peace with his or her money in terms of the obligation of Christian stewardship has failed a basic test of discipleship. Jonathan Swift, sometime dean of St. Patrick's Cathedral in Dublin, one day made a public appeal for a certain needy cause. He announced as his text, "He that giveth to the poor lendeth to the Lord." Then he said, in what was probably the shortest sermon of which there is record, "If you like the security, plank down the gold." That was all, but it was enough.

8. The layperson should pray daily for his or her pastor. It is hard to dislike or abuse anyone for whom we pray!

I have spoken earlier in this chapter about the responsibilities of United Methodism to its average laypeople. I have been speaking in this particular section about those reciprocal responsibilities that rest on church members where United Methodism is concerned. The professor of long ago days in Johnson City, Tennessee, whose story I told earlier, said, "I felt I *ought*." It is this *awareness of obligation* that distinguishes the authentic layperson in the Body of Christ.

George M. Ivey, one of the great merchant princes of our Southland and a humble layman in Providence United Methodist Church, Charlotte, North Carolina, happened to be the chairperson of that congregation's Pastor-Parish Committee when I was bishop in the area. He called my office to make an appointment and came to see me one afternoon. After a few pleasantries, he announced the purpose of his visit. "I have come," he said, "in my capacity as chairman of our church's Pastor-Parish Committee, and I am privileged in behalf of that committee to request that you return our pastor for another year. I have already spoken to the district superintendent." We talked a bit following this statement, commenting on this particular minister's qualities and his faithful service in his current appointment. Then I looked Mr. Ivey squarely in the eyes, for we were close friends, and asked him if the report which he had brought to me represented his personal viewpoint. He replied, smiling, "No, it does not. I happen to feel differently. But I believe it does represent the views of most of our congregation and certainly the judgment of the majority of our committee. I have presented our recommendation to you honestly, and I hope very sincerely that you will act upon it affirmatively."

Here was responsible leadership, the acceptance of obligation with integrity, even though Mr. Ivey himself thought otherwise. "I felt I ought."

A Personal Word

In my ministry I have tried to be a layperson's bishop. This has not been difficult for me, for I have found myself so deeply in debt to the splendid laypeople with whom God has surrounded me that I have an incurable sense of gratitude to them. There was a certain man in Chattanooga during my first pastorate, when I knew more than I have ever known since. This man came to the parsonage each Sunday after the evening service with a list of mistakes I had made in my two sermons that day. Often he was unable to finish his review without an extended session on Monday night. Sometimes his visits would irritate me, and there were days when I felt humiliation. But now, forty years later, it would be impossible for me to measure his helpfulness. He is still a dear friend and we visit occasionally.

In three of the annual conferences that I have served as episcopal leader, I have had Lay Advisory Councils. They were composed of forty or fifty laypeople chosen jointly by the Work Area on Lay Activities and myself. The conference lay leader, of course, was always a member, as were the presidents of United Methodist Women and United Methodist Men. There were millionaires, farmers, rural mail carriers, store clerks, professional people, Black and white, male and female. It was a completely unofficial fellowship drawn from all geographical parts of an annual conference. Sometimes the group voted on issues, but the result of the vote was binding on no one.

Members came to two day-long meetings every conference year, and I hosted a luncheon for them at each session. The only other clergy person present was my administrative assistant. I undertook to interpret to them the concerns that the bishop had for the annual conference, and they in turn interpreted to me the feelings of laypeople in the local churches. The Lay Advisory Council was particularly helpful to me when critical issues confronted the church and the conference.

In 1968 I had the privilege of appointing the first Black district superintendent in the Southeastern Jurisdiction, and before I undertook this important action I asked my Lay Advisory Council to discuss the matter in depth. I had explained all the reasons for my intention, but those were tense and difficult days and the conversation was heated. Finally, after hours of struggle between emotion and reason, a very prominent man, wealthy and influential throughout the state, arose and said, "It will surprise all of you for me to make this motion. But I have heard our bishop lay this matter upon our Christian consciences, as have you, and now I move that our informal body give him a unanimous vote of confidence as he carries out his announced plan, and that we reinforce that vote by returning to our communities and our districts and helping our neighbors and friends understand and accept what is happening." That vote, taken on a Saturday afternoon in Charlotte, became a firm foundation for the success of my subsequent action.

We have a long way to go as a church if we are to rekindle the fires of vigorous lay involvement at the grass roots of United Methodism, and a still longer way to go if we are to utilize in the fullest possible way the almost illimitable possibilities of an informed and dedicated laity. We who are clergy must convince our laypeople that *they are really important to us,* not simply as parishioners to be served, but as counselors to be heard. We must be willing to sit at the feet of those with whom we disagree, to expose our own viewpoints to theirs, and we must receive their input with open and grateful minds. They must be made aware of our *genuine respect* as well as our *pastoral love*. Our ministry to them must constitute a total outpouring of our hearts and minds and all the time required to meet their needs.

The first great layman I ever knew was my paternal grandfather, a farmer in Washington County, near Jonesboro, Tennessee. He was plain and, by today's standards, poor in this world's goods. A camp meeting was held in that lovely rural community each August, under a rustic shed with rough pews and a hand-hewn pulpit. One side of the crude chancel area with its hard benches was set apart as the "amen corner," and my grandfather always sat there, in his new camp meeting suit, with a few select comrades! He went to annual conference every year to represent his little church and to see that his beloved pastor was returned or a suitable replacement sent instead. One year he took me with him, and I got to meet the bishop, for Grandpa always managed to have a conversation with him before he left the seat of the conference! He loved his church, his family, and his little farm; he was unshakably loyal to his minister, and he believed that the only thing that really mattered in this life was the Christian faith. But he expected his church (even the bishop!) to respect him and hear him as one of its members, and he demanded of his preacher impeccable integrity, hard work, and the best sermons he was able to prepare. I think my deep respect for the laity of the church began long ago with my admiration for my grandfather, but it did not end there.

The church does not exist for its ministry. It exists for the laypeople, those who are in it now and those who will be in it in days and years ahead. With all my heart and soul I believe in laymen and laywomen. When they have an authentic experience of Jesus Christ and information about United Methodism which we who are their ministers are able to provide, our church will be safe in their hands. *Even if they change some things!*

CHAPTER THREE
Agony and Ecstasy in a Stained-Glass Jungle

Prologue

Mary Ann and I took a leisurely vacation trip through New England, accompanied by a friend and his wife. As we wandered through the beautiful northeastern states we had time for long thoughts and candid introspection.

One subject that occupied me in those days was the authenticity of my personal ministry. It was easy, in the presence of old friends, to go back to the early days when my call to preach was a fresh experience and my Christian idealism unspoiled by life's sometimes traumatic "middlescence." I remembered again that I entered the ministry because of what Jesus Christ had done for me and because of an overwhelming compulsion to share him with other human beings. In those days, the ultimate measurement of nearly every act in my daily work was how much it did to communicate the love of God to the people of my parish and beyond. I worked hard for little pay, but was never aware of any sacrifice on my part.

As we drove northward through Connecticut and Massachusetts and then across Vermont and New Hampshire into Maine, I kept asking myself if I still had the same quality of motivation and the same gratitude for the privilege of being in ministry. I remembered a fragment from a song I heard Homer Rodeheaver sing when I was a boy—"if your heart keeps right. . . ." If a minister's heart is not right, then it is wrong for him or her to expect the blessings of God. The sins of pride, arrogance, selfishness, and prejudice must come under the cleansing grace of our Lord, not once but again and yet again. Repenting, searching the Scriptures, and praying in simple, even childlike faith must characterize our times of reflection and devotion. We simply cannot share a Christ who is not genuinely and currently real to us. The erosion of administrative responsibility is a perennial peril for a parish minister, a connectional person, a district superintendent, or a bishop.

My musings during that trip made me increasingly aware of the sinfulness of *little* thoughts and moods. It is so easy, because we are human, to think negatively and to look for the worst in our fellow human beings, so easy to carry chips on our shoulders, and to react childishly to small injuries or grievances. When we do, the flavor of life sours and the context of our thinking and serving is suddenly a denial of the very gospel we have been ordained to proclaim. To be close to God is to overcome little thoughts and attitudes, to try to build perspectives that match his mountains and oceans in grandeur and sublimity. By the time we headed home, I had promised my own soul that I would get up in the mornings with positive, compassionate, and Christlike viewpoints toward my fellow human beings and my daily tasks.

About Being a Minister Today

It is *hard* to be a good minister of Jesus Christ in this moment of history, much harder than it was when I was ordained and began to serve my parishes. I think I know why.

During the years since I came into this episcopal position, I have had opportunity to sense the frustration and confusion that compose the climate in which the modern minister undertakes his or her work. The once prestigious image of the office of minister has vanished. In an earlier day the minister was the best informed person in a community and was viewed with immense respect and accorded automatic leadership. That day is over.

There are also other problems. The job of parish leader needs to be analyzed to reflect the minister's abilities and level of education. In spite of the better salaries now paid by our churches, a minister can command much more money doing something else, and still be engaged, generally speaking, in service to the human family. The minister's spouse is often involved in an identity crisis, not having experienced the same vocational certainty that has come to the minister, and therefore unable to offer the empathetic, loving assistance that should be expected from a helpmeet. Perhaps most disturbing of all, since the maladies of the world's secularism have invaded the ministry as well, the shadows of intellectual and spiritual doubt have brought a sad eclipse of faith to the minds of some in Christian service. Until they find answers to their own probing questions, their trumpets must give uncertain sounds.

Other impediments to successful ministry are less elegant. Bishop Jack Tuell, in a devotional address to the Baltimore General Conference, declared that if John Wesley and Francis Asbury were here today, they would bemoan the sloth and laziness of some of the preachers who occupy our pulpits. He suggested that certain ministers within our ranks are in danger of losing their sense of servanthood and sacrifice and most of us know this is tragically true. Let me develop a bit more thoroughly what I have tried to say.

I think the restlessness in the soul of the ministry today comes basically from one of three sources, or perhaps a combination among these three.

First, there is honest doubt about a minister's role in the new society and about ministerial influence with congregations which often are distressingly unwilling to consider the serious demands of discipleship as the preacher attempts to interpret them.

Second, and this is alluded to in a preceding paragraph, a ruthlessly materialistic society committed to science and agnostic reason has caught ministers off balance and has so affected their reading and thinking that old and meaningful experiences have been forgotten and deep and significant convictions eroded. Preachers so affected no longer have a thrilling gospel to proclaim with certainty, for doubts simply don't preach! To admit this, even within the sanctuary of one's own soul, would prove an intolerable embarrassment; hence, the minister often erects a structure of rationalization, the real function of which is to transfer the focus of the problem away from the condition of his or her own heart.

Third, and related to the second, although the minister has spoken against secularism faithfully for years, all the while that same secularism subtly and quietly has been invading the minister's own soul. He or she is the pathetic victim of the secular society against which carefully prepared sermons have declaimed vehemently. With the saturation of the minister's soul by material concerns, spiritual certainty has often vanished. Do we remember the haunting words of William Cowper?

>Where is the soul-refreshing view
>Where is the blessedness I knew
>When first I saw the Lord?
>Where is the soul-refreshing view
>Of Jesus and His word?
>   From "Walking with God"

A growing practice among United Methodist ministers, in radical contradiction to earlier custom, is the use of alcoholic beverages, certainly another evidence of capitulation to a secular age. Actually The United Methodist Church has never changed its strong basic position in opposition to drinking by clergy or laity, only reworded it and relocated it in the *Book of Discipline.* I regard a minister's acquiescence to this widespread social practice in our time as constituting dangerous relaxation of personal discipline, poor example-setting for his or her congregation and constituency, and a giant step in the direction of weakened Christian witness and compromised individual integrity. I cannot imagine this happening in a church *with our tradition* without affecting in a negative way a minister's own dedication and his or her understanding and presentation of the gospel.

There *may* be a *fourth* source of the preacher's unrest. We seem to see it often in cabinets. Every person has a ceiling above his or her capacities, but only the wise ones are able to know where it is or, indeed, that it is there at all. Therefore, some ministers expect continuing appointment advancements, sometimes even in the face of professional failures. They resent the promotion of classmates beyond their own levels of achievement, not recognizing that these classmates *may* have particular gifts and graces that are not part of their own endowments for ministry. True, at times the system favors a certain individual, or appears to, but ordinarily when this happens others may expect appropriate recompense in due season. However, the system cannot and should not be blamed when ministers' expectations exceed their abilities, nor can the system easily effect an adjustment in this sad inequity.

Let me illustrate with a story quite apart from the ministry. When I was a college president, novelist and poet May Sarton often came to our campus in lyceum programs. We became good friends during those years, and I recall vividly how one night after Miss Sarton had lectured on our campus a young man in the audience arose with a question. "How do you feel," he asked her, "about Ernest Hemingway?" I thought Miss Sarton's reply was important for ministers as well as others. "I like Mr. Hemingway's style of writing very much," she said. "But I preface all of my thinking about Ernest Hemingway by remembering that I do not have his ability. He was a genius and I am not. When I remember this, it becomes quite easy for me to appreciate Mr. Hemingway and to admire the superb writing which he has bequeathed to all of us."

What May Sarton said that evening would help many United Methodist ministers. It has helped me when I have been tempted to resent the fact that someone else was given a higher position or a more important privilege than I.

Ministers are human, and if we were not we could not possibly be good ministers. But over and beyond our humanness, we must look afresh at our commitment and determine in the candor of our own souls whether or not that commitment has suffered erosion. It may be necessary to look beyond the clever rationales that we sometimes have developed to justify our jealousies and self-centeredness. We quibble over salaries in the high thousands of dollars, when the early Methodist circuit rider burned out his life for sixty dollars a year (not even extravagant inflation negates this point). We are sometimes troubled over minor differences among luxurious parsonages when our Master had "nowhere to lay his head." The church will never strike a meaningful blow against secularism until the ministry itself is freed from materialism's icy grip. The wise reader will know that I am not justifying poor pay for preachers or poor housing for their families, but rather am indicating a malady of the soul that afflicts all of us and goes far deeper than figures or buildings.

The Matter of a Call

I realize that there are many times when I need to review and refresh my own sense of calling to the Christian ministry. As I ponder my situation and as I think of the calls that have come to other ministers who are my colleagues and friends, I recognize that God's voice summons us in vastly different ways. To some it comes suddenly, sharply, and with unmistakable clarity, often taking the form of a specific experience or event. It did not come to me that way. After my own acceptance of Jesus Christ as my personal Savior and Lord, which *was* a definite experience in my life, I worked my way gradually into my local church, surrounded on every hand by solicitous Christian friends who offered me love and encouragement. I spent much time praying and reading my Bible and other devotional literature. I went to hear great preachers and attended youth conferences. Gradually, almost imperceptibly, I became aware that I *must* preach, and one day—I cannot put my finger on when it was—I was conscious that my entire being was literally saturated with a sense of God's call.

Much of the genius and glory of the Christian ministry through the years is traceable to the fact that the man or woman involved has been certain of God's call to do the work. An overwhelming inner motivation, some holy compulsion quite beyond description, has slain petty grievances and caused even substantial sacrifices to seem insignificant. One saw it in the early church fathers, in the missionaries, in the pioneer circuit riders of our own denomination, and one sees it still in *many* deeply dedicated ministers who are controlled by high principle and impelled by the disciplines of a holy covenant. A modern world with its affluent society and all the accouterments of secularism has rendered such a brand of consecration awkwardly conspicuous, and some people with the sophisticated newer view suspect such ministers, accusing them of an outmoded naïveté instead of an enlightened intelligence. Probably it is normal to expect that many ministers, working in the context of today's world, will surrender, often unintentionally, to the kind of self-centered motivation that can destroy the glory of the Christian's calling.

In his spiritual autobiography, George Docherty speaks of the wonder of God's call to him:

> The knowledge of God's nearness breaks in upon life as a milk-white thread of lightning [that] illumines for one transient moment a night-dark landscape, revealing every tree, house and hill. Or as imperceptibly, but no less dramatically, as the first touch of spring or tang of winter. In this moment, one thing alone is known—this is God. . . . As the poetic eye sees earth's beauty and the sensitive ear detects the undergirding melancholy of the Beethoven string quartets, so to the soul that dares to believe God is, does God speak. . . . It happened [to me as I left for home from the office where I was employed] twenty-five years ago. Spring was in the evening air. The slanting rays of the setting sun reddened by the city haze touched with saffron the gray roofs of Glasgow. . . . My sudden, simple response to the realized love of God set me upon a long, long trail from a spring evening that now lies in the lee of the years. [For me,] life was never again to be the same. Quite simply I resolved to be a preacher.[1]

Have you and I, indeed, a sure calling? Does it supersede trivial matters and transcend material considerations? Has it been tarnished by the passing years, so that its loveliness and power are but memories? If these questions anger us, I plead that we inquire of our own souls if such anger is perchance a subconscious effort to avoid the truth about ourselves. For many of us, it is time to stop running from reality.

Appointment-making

The first time my appointment as a Methodist pastor was read by a bishop at an annual conference, I had no previous knowledge that I was even being considered for the church to which I had been named, and I couldn't find a living soul present at the annual conference who could tell me where the church was located, even though it was in the city of the conference sessions! My wife and I were staying at a boarding house not far from the host church, and neither of us will ever forget how we spent that night sitting on the side of a bed, alternately praying and weeping. When finally we found the church the next morning, it proved to be a seventy-five-year-old farmhouse located on a three-acre tract of land, with no parsonage and thirty-seven members. We were to live in the guest room of the board chairperson. Our salary had been cut from $2,700 to $1,300 and we were compelled to drop our life insurance. We wondered if we had been destroyed, but we were young and strong and hopeful—and God was good. We spent five deliriously happy years in that appointment, making hundreds of friends, building a beautiful new church, acquiring a spacious, lovely parsonage, and leaving for our successor a thriving congregation of six hundred members. When we go back there now, our hearts still rejoice over one of the supremely happy chapters in our total ministry.

Often, but not always, this is the story of United Methodist appointments. We learned in that experience that the attitude of the parsonage family has much to do with circumstances that develop. The wife of one of the district superintendents in the Charlotte Area put it strikingly: "Happiness," she said, "is the first thing we pack when we move to a new appointment!" To be sure, our system, upon occasion, can hurt preachers and churches—at least temporarily. Much of this, when it happens, is because of the *guaranteed appointment* provision in our law that promises every minister who behaves himself or herself a church, and every church a minister. There are always some preachers in an annual conference whom no church really wants, just as there are churches that no member of the conference would choose to serve. One solution might be to get the two together! However, when the inexorable arithmetic of the appointment process in the end decrees that *some* unfortunate assignments must be made in order to comply with the law under which we work, we should remember that such assignments are reviewed annually and can be corrected by a conscientious bishop and cabinet. I have always felt that certain parsonage families—such as those that have special problems of health and educational cost, together with ministers who have been either wronged or overlooked by the system—should have special priority whenever a new set of appointments is made. My practice has been to devote an early cabinet session to the careful hearing and consideration of authentic special cases, and I have found that several, although not all, of these can be helped each year.

Unquestionably, one of the most important of all responsibilities given to a bishop is that of making fair and satisfactory appointments; and also unquestionably, because of the intricate process involved, this can never be done perfectly. The bishop always finds that the reach far exceeds the grasp!

A bishop must never play favorites; especially is this true when he or she deals with good ministers who, for their own adequate reasons, have opposed the bishop at some point in his or her administration. A bishop must always be ready to reassess the qualities and abilities of a minister when new facts are presented and must never forget that ministers can and do change for the better! The only security a United Methodist preacher has is the integrity of his or her bishop and cabinet.

Special attention must be given to the accomplishment of interracial assignments and the placing of women clergy and clergy couples. Again, especially in the case of interracial assignments, reach often exceeds grasp. Success here requires persistent patience and intentional courage, but the bishop must keep working toward this goal if the scandal of a racist church is to be removed from the name of United Methodism in our time.

I have never acknowledged in my own thinking that a competent female minister is to be regarded as any different from a competent male minister, as far as appointment opportunity is concerned. I know that to many of our churches the idea of a woman preacher is still novel, but I have found in most cases that United Methodist laity are reasonable and can be persuaded by the bishop and/or district superintendent to accept the minister proposed regardless of sex.

It is long past time for our denomination to move beyond the problems of racism and sexism and be able to devote its energies to other issues. But I must be honest enough to confess my own failures here and reaffirm my determination to be a fairer and a more effective administrator in the time I have left.

The whole United Methodist system of deploying ministry seems to be opposed to the basic anti-authoritarian mood of our day. We *send* ministers instead of *calling* them. The consultative process is a useful effort to build a bridge between the two approaches to deployment and to make our method more acceptable than it would be otherwise in the modern United Methodist Church. It is a much needed and long overdue effort to correct the practice of harmful autocracy in the process of placing preachers. Consultation is now required by the law of our church, as it should be. It is never intended to mean that a minister, in the final analysis, can refuse a reasonable appointment or that a charge can decline a defensible projection for its pulpit. The bishop and the cabinet, in the end, have both the right and the obligation to make the appointments; otherwise, in our system, we would have chaos and vastly increased injustice. However, the consultative process, properly implemented, supplies an immense amount of information about preachers and churches which should guarantee appointments that are substantially fairer and of far better quality. Both parsonage families and churches are consulted in a genuinely Christian spirit before assignments are finalized. Intelligence, maturity, emotional balance, and absolute confidentiality are required to make the consultative process work and to keep it from becoming a maelstrom of hopeless, hurtful confusion. We have been given a meaningful technique to help us all achieve more equitable and defensible results in matching ministers with churches. We need to remember that it is never safe for human beings, ordained or unordained, who persist in thinking and acting like children, to play with such a delicate process as though it were a toy! Local churches, ministers, cabinets, and bishops are still in the learning process where the correct use of consultation is concerned.

A number of years ago the Council of Bishops, in a special

session under the leadership of Jesse R. DeWitt, developed basic steps to serve as consultation guidelines for all annual conferences in our church. It may be helpful to repeat them here in the somewhat recast form which I have used in my last two areas, based on Section VIII, paragraphs 529-533, pages 269-72, *The Book of Discipline,* 1984:

(1) The District Superintendent visits pastor and spouse to determine their thinking with regard to remaining another year or moving.

(2) The District Superintendent communicates with the local church's Pastor-Parish Relations Committee in order to discover the thinking and recommendations of this Committee with regard to the pastor's staying or moving. Usually a written instrument is introduced and explained to the Committee, and the Committee presents its views by marking this instrument appropriately.

(3) The District Superintendent reports the findings to the Cabinet, together with his or her recommendation.

(4) On the basis of all such recommendations, and with the help of carefully chosen data about both churches and pastors, the Cabinet "projects" appointments.

(5) The District Superintendent communicates *projections* to pastors and then to Pastor-Parish Relations Committees with the understanding that they are simply projections and at this point highly *tentative.* No pastor is to make contact with his or her projected new church, and no Pastor-Parish Committee is to contact any minister.

(6) If *new* information has emerged as the result of step #5, projections affected are reconsidered. If not, the Cabinet confirms the projections.

(7) The District Superintendent reports again to pastors and Pastor-Parish Committees. An optional "get acquainted" visit between the projected pastor and the proposed church is allowed, with the Cabinet's consent.

(8) The Cabinet engages in its final review of projections, with the understanding that any may still be changed at this point in the process.

(9) The Cabinet gives official notification to the pastor and the Pastor-Parish Committee.

(10) The tentative appointments are released for public information, but with the understanding that any appointment remains tentative until the Bishop confirms it at Annual Conference.

(11) All appointments are confirmed or fixed by the Bishop at the Annual Conference session.

United Methodists believe in the *sent* system. We all know that there are good denominations that have elected to use the *called* system. Obviously both methods have their assets and liabilities. It may be true that the called system is in position to favor the preacher of unusual ability and the church of affluent means. But we continue to believe in our *sent* system because it provides a pulpit for every worthy preacher and a minister for every congregation, enables the denomination to protect the career of the minister who has been courageous enough to do and say what is right, and provides the corrective possibility of an annual review.

Our final word here: I have come to believe that, where effective ministry is in progress, *longer* pastorates are important and right in this new day of shifting sociological and ecclesiastical conditions.

A Potpourri of Practical Suggestions for Ministers

The proper care and feeding of ministers can be a delicately complex proposition, but is always infinitely important. Anyone performing ministry effectively must be able to do it in the most favorable setting possible under the circumstances. God's call alone is not enough. Too, there are always an abundance of problems that cannot be escaped; therefore, a minister must try to identify unnecessary problems and learn how to avoid them.

From my own ministerial experience and the years I have been privileged to spend as a pastor of pastors, I have some suggestions.

1. *Protect your marriage and your family life.* A minister's home life may become his or her most effective sermon. Marriage is a partnership, but it takes two to make it so.

Intentional intellectual and spiritual growth together is a must if minister and spouse are to find mutual contentment in their Christian vocation. Private time together and regularly planned family experiences with the children should have priority. Thirty-one years of my own ministry have involved assignments requiring nearly constant travel away from home, and my greatest regret, in retrospect, is that I could not spend enough time with our son during his early and impressionable years; something that never can be corrected now.

A wholesome and satisfying sex life is important. Happily, one of the *positive* results of the sexual revolution has been to lift sex out of the old Victorian negativistic context and to recognize it, within the marital relationship, as one of the beautiful gifts of a good God. From my own counseling experience with parsonage families in all of the annual conferences I have served, I would say that sexual difficulties constitute one of three major problem areas related to clergy divorce. The other two are shared motivation for ministry and family finance.

Another observation I have made from my exposure to ministerial families is that the early, compassionate, and *discreet* concern of annual conference officials for parsonage marriages in trouble would result in saving many of them. The extraordinary tensions and pressures converging upon minister and spouse in today's church and world must be recognized as an incontrovertible fact of modern life, and far more elaborate and expensive preventive and corrective measures than the church has heretofore attempted must be undertaken.

A good literature for parsonage couples has been developed in recent years. One of several books which my wife and I like to recommend is Ruth Truman's practical and down-to-earth volume entitled *Underground Manual for Ministers' Wives*[2] (now out of print). In addition there is *What's Happening to Clergy Marriages?* by David and Vera Mace (Abingdon Press, 1980).

2. *Make yourself the most attractive person possible.* I mean good grooming, for to dress carelessly is inexcusable for a

representative of Jesus Christ. I mean especially the use of correct grammar, for there are men and women with fine education, splendid thought, and deep dedication whom cabinets have great difficulty placing in responsible assignments because they are persistently and inexcusably inaccurate in their use of the English language. They have never learned how to make subjects and predicates agree, and they invariably follow prepositions with the wrong case! I mean also disposition. It is tragic when a bad temper or an ungracious attitude interferes with ministry. The achievement of important goals such as these lies within reach of anyone acceptable as a member of an annual conference, but steady discipline and hard work are required.

3. *Pay your debts.* A good credit rating in the community is a positive part of any minister's image. I know there are times when circumstances make this practice impossible, but one can always go to his or her creditors with an honest explanation and work out a mutually satisfactory plan for eventual payment. It helps also for a husband and wife to make and honor a budget that enables the family, even at some temporary sacrifice, to live within its income!

4. *Visit your people.* Next to asking for a good preacher, Pastor-Parish Committees may be expected to request a faithful pastor. Recent generations of ministers often have denied the importance of this function, I fear sometimes with seminary endorsement. My experience as a pastor, as well as in this office, has led me to believe that this constitutes a major mistake. I believe in a moderate use of office hours for scheduled counseling, but I am certain that office time never replaces the importance of visitation in hospital and homes—and not just when people experience sickness or bereavement. Visiting today is more difficult because of the advent of high-rise apartment buildings and other secured housing, and also because of people's varied schedules and full calendars. It may require making specific appointments, but the sincere pastor can still arrange to see church members either at home or at their places of business. A visit by a minister should

have a spiritual purpose, but sensitive intelligence always should guide the decision about offering prayer or reading from the Bible.

5. *Struggle to avoid at all costs the shadow of scandal over your life.* We are human, all sinners saved by grace, and our church imposes on us the dangerous duty of visiting from house to house. This exposes us to all kinds of potentially compromising circumstances and occasionally a difficult situation will arise, but ordinarily this is one of the problems a minister can avoid by exercising sufficient care. There are some homes where one should visit only with one's spouse. I remember in my early pastoral assignments calls came at night and had to be answered. On several occasions my wife and I took our baby boy to the next-door neighbors and went together to such places. Counseling, in my own ministry, has always been done with the office door slightly ajar and when someone else is in the building. Common sense rules can go far to avert sorrow and damage.

6. *Buy books and engage in disciplined study.* Ministers encounter two great enemies at this point: their own laziness, from which not even sanctification can exempt them, and the trivial demands people make on their time. Intellectual growth is arduous, and books are expensive.

Erasmus wrote to a friend in Paris centuries ago, "When I can get hold of some money, I'll buy the Greek authors and afterwards some clothing." You don't need extensive formal learning in order to be an educated preacher (although I favor it whenever possible), for education has never been confined to an institution. It is a love affair that exists between an individual and great books and ideas, and it can be carried on anywhere and always.

7. *Never become objectionably professional.* The ministry should employ at all times the highest type of professional ethics and etiquette. However, I refer to something quite different. My friend Myron Augsburger hints at this point very well when he insists that a minister should avoid using "the

language of Canaan." Pious preacher patter is passé in our day and, as has been said elsewhere in these pages, the unctuous tones of a one-time typical minister definitely do not belong to the latter part of the twentieth century. However, there is something still more important. When a pastor goes into a grief-stricken home, he or she would do well, if it is sincere, to weep a little. Too ready an eloquence can sound to heartbroken people like the pronouncement of a clerical automaton. It can have the hollow ring of emptiness. It would be far better to grope for the right word and falter and stumble and have to start again, for then the grieving people would sense the minister's identification with their own great need. I have always felt that I must avoid becoming mechanical or objectionably professional in my pastoral care, or I would not be worth very much in the ministry of the Lord Jesus Christ.

8. *Cultivate high ministerial ethics.* I remember Bishop Hughes speaking to my class coming into full connection and saying one particular thing: "When you leave a place, for God's sake, leave it!" We would have a far more effective and pleasant itinerancy if we would endeavor to practice that counsel faithfully. I have helped in weddings and funerals only at the present pastor's invitation, and I have always tried to telephone him or her if my wife and I contemplated a visit in that parish.

I have always watched myself at another point where failure is easy and natural. I have tried never to develop a critical attitude toward my brothers and sisters in the ministry. I don't tear a sermon apart; I don't analyze it. I am not a professor of homiletics. When I hear a fellow minister preach the gospel, I try to remember that I am only a Christian sitting in a pew in need of spiritual help. These are simply acts of kind courtesy—the proper type of professionalism.

9. *Keep jealousy out of your heart.* Sometimes appointments appear to be disappointments. There probably is no United Methodist preacher alive who has served very long without traveling that road. Fortunately, many of these initial "disappointments" turn out a bit later to be God's appoint-

ments. I wish Pastor-Parish Committees as well as ministers would remember this. If a Christian minister ever allows the hobgoblins of prestige and money or the demons of human jealousy to conquer his or her soul, that minister is sure to lose the happiness, the peace, the excitement and the wonder of ministry and that is a terrible price to pay. The person who falls into this trap has made a bad swap!

10. *Keep your dreams fresh.* Years ago I heard Robert Elliott Speer, the great Presbyterian architect of missions, say to a group of young people, "We must rediscover the romance of following Christ." We have to do that constantly. We get mixed up sometimes and let the wrong motivations creep into our lives and thoughts. Have you ever read anything that came from Arthur Wentworth Hewitt's pen? He spent his ministry in a rural setting, but preached and wrote with such shining eloquence and excited passion about the glory of his service in the countryside that anyone who heard or read him wondered why a person ever bothered to preach in the cities! That is what I am talking about: seeing *every* new assignment as a fresh opportunity to help God do his wonderworks, and nurturing constantly that moving sense of mission that helps dwarf even the most unfortunate outward circumstances. Hewitt lived and died believing that his had been the happiest and most magnificent ministry in the history of our church. He wrote about it in that exquisite piece of Americana entitled *The Old Brick Manse.*[3]

It is easy to have dreams as a young minister, but it is hard to keep them from being tarnished as time goes by. To cling to them into one's senior years, in spite of the ravages of cynicism and bitterness, is an epic accomplishment. But the truth is that we are closer to the real meaning and glory of Christian ministry when we are young and our dreams are fresh than we ever are afterward. I would move heaven and earth to retain my personal *vision splendid*!

11. *Keep your prayer life vigorous and strong.* Years ago as a seminary student I became confused and thought I was losing my faith. I had discovered that Moses did not write all the

Pentateuch and that Isaiah was a family. I packed my things one night and planned to leave the university. I didn't know where I was going but I was on my way, except that I had no money to buy a bus ticket! I went up and down the dormitory halls trying to borrow a few dollars, but no one would lend anything to me, so I unpacked.

The next day I went to see my seminary dean Henry Burton Trimble. I unfolded my story to him as he listened patiently for an hour. He made no comment at all on anything I had said, but he looked at me a long, long moment and asked, "Earl, how is your prayer life?" In the years since then, when I have been bewildered I have often remembered the dean's question, "How is your prayer life?" This is the battlefield on which a person's ministry ultimately is won or lost.

Bishop Gerald Kennedy in his Lyman Beecher lectures told about his own first year in the ministry. Everything was awry. The bishop had sent him to the wrong place. His wife was unhappy. There wasn't really an opportunity. The salary was low. Suddenly he realized that his attitude must change, or he would have to get out of the ministry. He began to think very seriously about some other vocation where he could invest his service. Then he realized that God had a stake in his ministry, too, and it was his task and responsibility to do what was right, to be faithful, to preach the gospel, and to *leave the rest with God*. It was then that he prayed. He said when once he "shifted into gear," he got along all right for the rest of his life as a pastor.[4] The message is a clear one for any of us who are ministers.

A Concluding Word

A position paper issued by the United Church of Canada a number of years ago began with this sentence: "The principal problem of the church in our time is its ministry." On some days I have found myself in agreement with that cryptic declaration, but on more days I have disagreed with it. It makes a minister like me, however, face up to my responsibility and take careful inventory of my motivation, spiritual growth, personal discipline, willingness to work hard, and commitment to the

Lord Jesus Christ. Surely those of us upon whom "the mighty ordination of the pierced Hands"[5] has fallen could make a substantive difference in the health of the church today, if we were willing to be and to do what is required.

The glorious part of it is that we would not be alone in our efforts. James S. Stewart, to whom I refer so frequently, stated this brief paragraph in the last sermon I heard him preach in Edinburgh: "Bring everything you have and are to your ministry—bring it without reserve. But when you have brought it, something else remains. Stand back, and see the salvation of God!"

CHAPTER FOUR
Theology and Doxology

Just before his sudden death, I encountered Carlyle Marney outside his Interpreters' House office at Lake Junaluska, North Carolina. He invited me in for a talk. As all of us who knew and loved him were aware, a conversation with Marney usually meant listening to what he wanted to say. This occasion was no exception. As he sat behind his desk puffing on his perennial pipe, he began to discuss *sin* and *grace*. He went on and on in his rich, inimitable way, and I was fascinated. Finally I began to laugh.

He stopped short in the middle of a sentence. "What are you laughing at?" he asked, almost brusquely.

"I'm laughing at you," I replied.

He bristled. "Why?" he shot back at me.

"Because, whether you realize it or not, you sound like an old-fashioned Baptist preacher—far more fundamentalist than I've ever been."

His eyes shot bolts of fire through me, and he stared belligerently. Then, quite suddenly, his expression softened and became quizzical. He leaned back in his chair and blew smoke rings into the air. "You know, Earl," he said, "you may be right, you just may be right."

That is my last memory of a dear friend and one of the seminal religious thinkers of our Southland. But it will never leave me because it confirmed earlier intimations I had experienced of a basic historical orthodoxy that Marney's facile mind had chosen to package, perhaps for purposes of communication, in heterodox wrappings. I have always been glad that our final conversation was about sin and grace—both rudimentary faith subjects.

United Methodists, along with people of other mainline Christian communions, passed through a period when *we almost lost our gospel.* The theological aridity that followed the collapse of liberalism, the gradual decline of continental and American neoorthodoxy, the ascendancy of existentialism and the appearance of radical theology with its insistence on the death of God made the thought-life of our church a parched desert where few if any of faith's flowers were able to survive or blossom. The fact that our denomination, particularly in the United States, has never been primarily a reflective Christian body, plus the dramatic surfacing of critical social issues following World War II, propelled us into an aggressive activism that left little time to recover theological foundations.

Old categories such as "liberal," "conservative," "modernist," "fundamentalist" became conspicuously obsolete. Theology was groping for new boundary lines, new meanings, and there were no great original American theological giants to guide the quest. My own impression was that we were dimly conscious of sitting and listening in some great philosophical concert hall where a chorus of *European* religious voices sang their stimulating, exciting, but often doleful music, more frequently in dissonance than in harmony. The soloists were artists named Barth, Brunner, Berdyaev, Tillich, Bultmann, and someone called Pierre Teilhard de Chardin, while standing far back in the chorus line were younger performers named Moltmann, Pannenberg, Ellul, and Thielicke. Guest artists from abroad included two brothers named Niebuhr. However, in retrospect, one wonders if these were the real religious thinkers of the period. Or if the more influential ones may not have been a coterie of irreverent amateurs, wearing casuals rather than clericals, people such as Albert Camus, Jean Paul Sartre, Ayn Rand, Ernest Hemingway, Hugh Hefner, Dylan Thomas, and James Baldwin. It was a time of nearly hopeless theological confusion (even though an earlier fundamentalism persisted in some circles), the product of a bold revival of antinomianism and hedonism, both impressively supported by the letters and arts of the day. Looming large in the background was that difficult-to-define and more-difficult-to-evaluate philosophical formulation known as *existentialism,* with its tempting array of partial truths and its interpretive cloak of many colors. A cloud of secular humanism was descending over the world, and church leadership was too close to events to be fully aware of what was happening. The resulting thought-life of the church, an interim adjustment to these pressures, seemed at times to deify the idea of human freedom and individuality to the point of risking moral relativism and inviting virtual elimination of a positive ethic. In practical terms, the new so-called theology was bound to encounter difficulty in attempting to undergird a philosophy of missions, a program of evangelism, or a serious effort to apply principles of righteousness to solidly entrenched social evils. Our false impression, strong in the late 1940s and early 1950s, that we were living in a day of religion's roseate renaissance, was abruptly over.

But vacuums never last. The movement of God's Spirit, making use of awakening Christian leadership in all communions and nations, brought the beginnings of a *new evangelicalism*. Its historical development was intriguing: much of it came as reaction to the old fundamentalism that had persisted during the arid era just described, and some of it came as an effort to inform the life of faith again with a basic doctrinal content that had all but vanished before humanism's onslaughts. In its pure form, the evangelical awakening struggled from its inception, and struggles still, to define an acceptable platform for its constituents, particularly where a clear doctrine of the Bible was concerned. Persistent although quiet in-fighting within its ranks and determined resistance to anything emerging from the Enlightenment probably dulled the total impact of the movement upon the general Christian community and damaged its image with many leaders whose roots were in the liberal tradition. But in spite of all this, directly and indirectly, the evangelical renaissance began to influence not only Protestantism but Roman Catholicism as well. Especially was this so when its more progressive leaders, including Carl F. H. Henry and Ronald J. Sider, called for an aroused social consciousness and a bold application of gospel principles to the suffering world. Dr. Henry wrote:

> If in its own ranks the church even now unduly esteems the mighty and the affluent at the expense of the weak and the poor,

and bows to the preferences, prerogatives and programs of the specially privileged, it can hardly hope to signal good news in countries where those rich in power and property exploit the underprivileged masses. . . . If wicked political regimes require what God forbids or disown what God commands, then the Christian community may not espouse an ethic of political neutrality and social non-involvement.[1]

It should be pointed out, particularly to United Methodists, that one of the indirect results of the evangelical awakening is a new focus upon the importance of the teachings of our own spiritual founder John Wesley. To be sure, the recently observed bicentennial of our church in the United States was also an important factor in creating fresh interest in Wesley's theology. I believe it is the kind of evangelicalism that reflects Wesley's own incredibly rich repertoire of Christian convictions that our church so desperately needs today. This would correct those unfortunate aberrations that some evangelical expressions have espoused in recent years and would bring the mind and heart of our church back to what Bishop Arthur J. Moore liked to call the *central certainties.*

Some years ago, former Yale dean Colin W. Williams, in his significant book *John Wesley's Theology Today,*[2] listed the great doctrines generally associated with Wesley's preaching and teaching, including the following: *prevenient grace, repentance* and *justification by faith,* the *atonement,* the *work of the Holy Spirit in new birth and assurance,* the *doctrine of the church, Christian perfection,* and *eschatological redemption.* They offer an abundance of preaching material for the lifetime of any faithful Wesleyan pulpiteer, and they constitute the kind of solid theological substance which, served up intelligently and convincingly, would inform the membership of our denomination with new knowledge and inspiration.

The evangelical awakening continues—and grows. It is beginning to settle itself into the prevailing Christian perspectives of the late 1980s. Unfortunately some denominational leaders and some seminary teachers have not yet acknowledged its reality or its strength. It has not been difficult for me to do so, even though I was trained in the old liberal tradition of Methodist seminaries in the 1940s. A conversation I had with

Theology and Doxology

Bishop Edwin Holt Hughes, a giant of our church and the whole Christian community, alerted me early in my ministry to the need for maintaining a balance of both liberal and conservative traditions in my theological reading. Combined with this, as I stated more fully in an earlier book, was the realization of my indebtedness to the loving-kindness and abiding interest in my welfare that a choice group of fundamentalist Christians gave me when I was an adolescent. It was one of the most precious gifts I have ever received.

An ecumenical student movement at the state university where I studied afforded me opportunity to have personal contact with such people as Dr. Howard Atwood Kelly, George W. Truett, Peter Marshall, Robert E. Speer, Grace Livingston Hill, Frank Gabelein, and the unforgettable British evangelist Gipsy Smith, Sr. The years of my early ministry brought me into contact with John R. Mott, Sherwood Eddy, C. S. Lewis, Ralph Spaulding Cushman, and Roy Hunter Short.

Even since I came into this office, I have had the enviable joy of knowing James S. Stewart, Archbishop Fulton J. Sheen, Carl F. H. Henry, Albert C. Outler, and Billy Graham, whose recent courageous stand for nuclear disarmament has placed the entire Christian community more deeply in his debt. I have sat also at the feet of great liberal leaders including A. J. Muste, Henry Sloane Coffin, Frederick Herzog, Wyatt Akin Smart, and Reinhold Niebuhr. I have long been grateful to God for the theologically eclectic background of my own life and ministry.

Because of my conviction that our theological uncertainty has played a major role in United Methodism's recent problems and in its membership decline, let me speak frankly of *four* areas of concern which lie heavily on my own conscience as an episcopal leader in our denomination.

Situation Ethics

Mainline Protestantism, perhaps still the most formidable force in molding contemporary America, currently is thrashing about in a quagmire of bewilderment and equivocation born of its inability to understand fully the world in which it serves and born also of its own gradual, often uncritical capitulation to certain theological and biblical perspectives that have roamed the religious scene in pleasant disguise for half a century. One of these perspectives is *situation ethics,* defined two decades ago by an Episcopal cleric named Joseph Fletcher, author also of a sensitive, almost devotional biography of the late Archbishop William Temple. Perhaps unconsciously it was an effort to accommodate the Christian faith to culture's new morality. With its amazing impact upon liberal Christian thought, it has threatened to take away the disciple's clear concept of the difference between right and wrong as delineated in Holy Scripture. As Dean Robert Fitch of the Pacific School of Religion pointed out years ago, it is based largely upon the idolatry of secularism and fails adequately to consider either the facts of sin and suffering or the meaning of the cross of Jesus Christ.[3]

It was the ready acceptance of this persuasive celebration of conditional human liberties more than anything else that caused otherwise committed followers of Jesus to play into the hands of the modern sexual revolution and to develop a sanctified tolerance for the ethical and moral disarray of the 1960s, 1970s, and 1980s all the way from Watergate to multiplied congressional scandals, and to a seriously compromised Christian view of human sexuality.

I am aware, of course, that Christian ethical thought now has moved quite beyond Fletcher's formulation, even though as yet no really improved system has taken definite shape. But, although situation ethics has become an out-of-date term, its far-reaching influence remains a part of the contemporary scene that cannot be ignored.

I am far from being a Puritan or a prude, but I still believe in the Ten Commandments. Furthermore, I am convinced that for the Christian who accepts the teaching of the New Testament, *there has never been, in fact, a moral revolution.* The unapologetic restoration of the principles of purity and integrity in the personal life of Christians, ordained or unordained, would go a long way toward reviving our church and reversing its decline. Nor does it need to result in an obnoxious piosity.

THEOLOGY AND DOXOLOGY

A Low Doctrine of the Bible

It is my conviction that many maladies characteristic of our denomination in the 1980s are traceable to the plain, simple, and extremely unfortunate fact that, gradually across recent years, we have compromised our earlier understanding of the Bible as God's Word.

Let me affirm two things about my own religious philosophy here. I do not accept the various theories of scriptural inerrancy. I am opposed to anything that smacks of bibliolatry. Second, I am grateful for the facts and insights that reverent critics and scholars have brought to our understanding of the Bible since near the end of the nineteenth century. Such people as George Adam Smith, S. R. Driver, and in modern days James S. Stewart and Hugh Anderson, have been able without intellectual dishonesty to accept the gifts of sound biblical scholarship and still to embrace Scripture as the Word of God. William Barclay, the popular Bible expositor from the University of Glasgow, put it in an interesting way:

> The supreme importance of the Bible is that in it and nowhere else we find Jesus Christ. Without it we would have no record of either the life or the teaching of Jesus. It may be claimed that even without the Bible we would have the tradition of the Church; but it is the Bible which prevents the distortion of that tradition. It is the touchstone; it is the assurance that no man can pervert the facts or invent new facts, for Jesus Christ is there.
>
> I believe that the Bible is the word of God because in it alone we confront him who was uniquely the Word of God.[4]

An examination of the position of Wesley at this point could constitute overdue therapy for our church. Let me quote a single paragraph from him:

> I have thought, I am a creature of a day, passing through life, as an arrow through the air. . . . I want to know one thing, the way to Heaven: how to land safe on that happy shore. God Himself has condescended to teach the way; for this very end He came from Heaven. He hath written it down in a book! O give me that

book! At any price, give me the book of God! I have it: here is knowledge enough for me.[5]

Wesley was always *homo unius libri,* a man of one book. For him, and for me, the fundamental teachings of the Holy Bible are not to be disregarded or rationalized away by arguing that the Good Book was a volume belonging to its own time and is really incompetent to speak to ours! I believe, in the language of our own Articles of Religion, that "the Holy Scripture containeth all things necessary to salvation" and that both its general and specific teachings concerning human morals and ethics are to be regarded as determinative in the understanding of God's will for all of us. For example, we dare not set aside the clear positions of the Bible on matters related to human sexuality simply to accommodate the Christian faith to contemporary life-styles. Nor dare we miss Scripture's unequivocal call to discipleship with its relentless insistence on sacrifice and unselfishness as we contemplate our own commitment to the holy life in the Lord's service. Modern biblical scholarship at its best never requires that Christians surrender their belief in a God who is almighty and miracle-working, transcendent as well as immanent.

I reject any interpretation of the Bible as a book of magic, but with all my heart and mind I do believe in the divine inspiration of Holy Scripture. When I have approached it as a student and mastered scholarship's discoveries about it, I can still come to it devotionally and, in a manner too simplistic for some, regard its sacred pages as containing God's love letters to me. I am convinced that God took the "initiative to inspire certain people to write down what was on his great heart for his children."[6] We United Methodists believe in revealed religion and it would be difficult to retain this belief without that sacred Book which leads us into the presence of the Living Word, the Lord Jesus Christ.

Reclaiming, with intelligence and spiritual purposefulness, a *high* doctrine of the Bible would bring our church far down the road to the solution of its other problems.

Unquestionably it is time for Wesley's followers today to exalt his insistence upon the primacy of Scripture and to become once more a *people of one book.*

The Loss of the Eternal Dimension

For a period of years our pulpits were virtually silent about the eternal dimension of the gospel. Surely this silence was related to the humanistic denial of the supernatural aspects of revealed religion. We revised the framework of our Christian thinking so that it became habitual for us to omit the concept of eternity and its implications. This was nearly a fatal mistake, with tragic ramifications.

The incendiary influence of the moral revolution on civilized life has been incalculable if not incomprehensible. It goes back to the old problem of the relation between morality and religion. Able, even stellar minds have denied that there is, or ought to be, any relation at all. Among these have been such people as Robert G. Ingersoll in our own country, and H. G. Wells, Arnold Bennett (in spite of his rearing in British Methodism), Sir Samuel Romilly, and Edward Clodd in England. To begin to name the more modern personalities who have espoused this divorcement between human action and religious commitment would be to undertake a nearly endless task. One flaw in their reasoning is that these people seem never to have examined honestly the causal effect of permeating historical and environmental religious influences upon their own often high moral convictions. Let me suggest two considerations.

First, deep belief in eternity is a major incentive for accepting God's redemption and cultivating a life whose quality conforms to the idea of a heaven. Jesus Christ consistently saw human beings as intended for a world requiring health of soul for its existence, and he saw those same human beings enslaved by sin. That was what sent him to the cross. This mighty transaction made God's forgiving and empowering love available to sinful men and women. Every day we are confronted by the necessary choice between good and evil. When we choose good, we fashion our own characters in harmony with our future environment, and when we choose evil we render ourselves less able to share any life where Christ reigns. Conviction that life does not end with what we call death is, indeed, a strong motivation in human determination to prepare for citizenship in a better world beyond this one.

Now consider another idea perhaps currently heterodox. A patently unbiblical anthropology in recent decades has resulted in human beings coming to regard themselves as creatures of time alone, rather than citizens of eternity. The idea of ultimate accountability in a moral creation and before a just and righteous Creator for deeds done on earth has largely been dismissed. The concept of judgment is no longer a frightening thought.

Jonathan Edwards' great sermon "Sinners in the Hands of an Angry God" would find few receptive auditors today. Multitudes of people either assume that death ends it all or embrace some vague idea of universalism. I reject these positions. To me, the higher anthropology of Scripture requires belief that a human being is made to live forever, and thus, even in spite of the gift of salvation, is accountable to Almighty God for his or her deeds in the flesh.

The explosive power of recovering this conviction would help destroy the dangerous idea that a person is free to do wrong provided he or she can escape apprehension. I know that love is always the supreme motivation of good religion, but I still believe that a proper fear of God has its place, particularly in an age of terrorism, organized crime, and other tragic products of human depravity.

However, our Christian faith in life eternal is not simply the idea of living forever, for this is essentially quantitative and can be pagan. Our New Testament belief is based wholly on the fact of the resurrection. God accepts our death and brings life out of death. Unbelievers are judged for their deeds in this life; believers, while under the grace of Christ, still are evaluated qualitatively for their works here.

We need the truth of eternity to reinforce our moral structures. Certainly there are other obvious arguments for recovering the dimension of eternity in our Christian thinking and preaching. But I have chosen to emphasize a reason pragmatically related to the here and now, the way to find a trail back to moral sanity, for my urgent plea that we reinstate the lost emphasis of the gospel's eternal dimension in United Methodism.

Liberation Theology

Liberation theology, a thought-system with many faces, often not accurately understood, began to emerge in recognizable form in the mid-1960s. We are familiar with it, for the most part, as Black theology, feminist theology, Latin American theology, and in its primarily European expression as the theology of hope (associated principally with the name of the German theologian Jürgen Moltmann). An early architect of this system was Gustavo Gutiérrez, a liberal Roman Catholic who used Marxist analysis in social diagnosis and who taught in the United States.

In Europe the liberation movement also has been known as political theology. Some of the European expressions, perhaps especially Moltmann's, were widely influenced by the late Ernst Bloch, an atheist and Marxist of Jewish descent.

In our country, at the present time, Dorothee Sölle, a member of the faculty at Union Theological Seminary in New York City, has written and lectured extensively on political theology and is a well-known expositor of the liberation viewpoint. Professor Frederick Herzog of Duke University has written a major book on liberation theology, using the whole of John's Gospel to reinforce his arguments and focusing especially on its eschatological dialectic of the present-future.

The Latin American expression of liberationism, one of the most prominent and influential, is often associated with the name of José Miguez Bonino (himself a Methodist), but there are others who have stood with him in the development of this extremely important version of liberation theology in today's world.

The foes of this system of thought have included such names as Michael Novak, Carl F. H. Henry (who balances his conviction that liberation theology violates scriptural Christianity with an equally strong insistence that Christianity must take an activist role against the abuse of the poor), Richard John Neuhaus, Peter Berger, and Paul Ramsey. A list of its critics, not its foes, would name Albert C. Outler.

An overly simple definition of liberation theology would insist that faithfulness to the gospel requires solidarity with the poor and the oppressed, and that the duty of a Christian is to apply the teachings of Jesus and the strength of the church to bring freedom, justice, and equality to the downtrodden of the earth, all the while seeking to remove from political and economic systems the root causes of oppression, injustice, and inequality. It is a theology of reformation and, in some instances, of revolution. The emergence of the problems of the developing countries has catapulted liberation theology into its present prominence.

It has made a nearly incredible impact, consciously and subconsciously, on the modern church—and surely on United Methodism. It is heavily reflected in the philosophy currently prevalent in our General Board of Global Ministries and to some extent in other general boards, in the teaching of our seminaries, and in the perspectives of the Christian conciliar movement.

Its biblical roots are undeniable and range across the entire length of Scripture. The Exodus theme is widely used, with such texts as Exodus 2:24-25; 3:9 ff.; 6:6; 15:1-2, 19:4-5; 22:21-24. Other Old Testament texts would include Deuteronomy 10:12–11:17; Amos 2:6-7, 10-11; 8:5-6; 9:7-8; Jeremiah 5:26-28; 22:13-14; Micah 6:8; Isaiah 1:10-20; 3:13-15; 42:1-4; 61:1-2; Psalm 72:12-14; Proverbs 19:17. I have already mentioned Hertzog's interpretation of the Fourth Gospel. It should also be said that Jesus' life generally is appealed to, especially his association with the poor and the lowly, his death as a subversive, and the cross as God's ultimate identification with sinners and the forsaken of the world. There are supporting passages, of course, in Luke, Matthew, and Mark. Other references would include I John 4:7-8; II Corinthians 8:9; Revelation 22.

There are many questions to be raised if one is to understand the real nature of liberation theology and comprehend the reasons it has become a divisive force in the North American United Methodist Church. I am not a student, much less a scholar, in this complicated field of study. However, the professors with whom I have had conversations, reinforced by the considerable number of books I have either read or examined, have made clear to me, that quite beyond the system's insistence upon Christian identification with the poor and the oppressed, liberationism makes use, in varying measures, of Karl Marx's critique of society and, generally speaking, espouses a socialistic economy over what we in this country know as capitalism. However, it would not be fair to say that all liberationists advocate the overthrow of capitalism, or that they are always uncritical of all aspects of Marxist thought. Some, Moltmann for example, say openly that Western nations will never be willing to abandon their cherished personal freedoms in order to achieve a certain pattern of economic justice.

Developing in recent years, largely under the leadership of such people as Orlando E. Costas, an evangelical scholar with roots in the developing world, is a version of liberation theology attractive to the so-called evangelical contingent of the Christian community. And many of the liberationists who are leaders in the Latin American version of this thought-system are themselves *theological* evangelicals whose personal Christian lives often reflect the principles of religious pietism.

Perhaps, as much as any other aspect of contemporary thought prevalent in United Methodism today, the concepts of liberation theology, often inadequately explained and understood, have contributed to *divisiveness* in the denomination. As has been said, much of the crisis of confidence where the work of the General Board of Global Ministries is concerned is traceable to the Board's apparently dedicated acceptance of the precepts of the liberationist movement. In fairness to the General Board of Global Ministries, it would be well for our church to be informed accurately and fully as to what version of liberation theology the Board accepts and promotes, particularly the extent of its acceptance of Marxist thought and its perspective toward socialism as opposed to capitalism. It would be well for our church to know if it believes that capitalism can be altered and improved in such a manner as to satisfy the liberationists' concern for the poor and the oppressed. The point here has direct reference to the 1984 Episcopal Address's call for the Board to demonstrate "that its staff is committed to Wesleyan theology."

Because of the undeniable present importance of the liberationist school of thought in United Methodist Church life, let me offer some personal observations about it.

1. The basic tenet of liberation theology is everlastingly biblical and right: the church *must* identify with the poor, the oppressed, the disinherited of the earth, and it must do so more courageously and effectively than ever before.

2. We should applaud with thanksgiving the attempt liberation theology makes to shift the focus of institutional religion from the conservation of ecclesiastical structures and the preservation of the status quo's seductive luxury to the primitive disciplines of early Christianity and its dedicated obsession to accomplish the transformation of individual and community life.

3. We who are older and more traditional must not dismiss liberation theology as apostasy with cavalier haste. It is very close to the mind and heart of the Savior in its purposes, and one reason we are critical and intolerant of it is that it places us under conviction for our churchly sins. Liberation theology itself, as a theological thought-form, is new. It is still in its developmental period, although Martin Marty alludes to "the prime years of the theology of hope" as being in the past.[7] If it is able *to criticize itself,* it will change—and hopefully for the better.

4. In my own opinion, liberation theology defeats its own high purposes (except in certain countries with existing socialist structures) in those instances where it uncritically accepts Marxist teachings and insists that justice and freedom can come only when capitalism is replaced by socialism. Let me give three supporting thoughts:

    A. The religion of Jesus Christ, I deeply believe, properly sits in judgment on *all* political and economic systems, rather than chooses one over another. Each has its faults, its failures.

B. Quite apparently, many examples of state socialism today pose grave threats to personal liberty and to economic stability and growth (a point first made by the Austrian economist Ludwig von Mises sixty-five years ago); and an increasing number of such countries, China and the Soviet Union, for example, are now employing a semblance of capitalism in order to survive. Archbishop Dom Helder Camara of Brazil said, "I am a socialist. . . . But I don't see the solution in the socialistic governments that exist today. . . . The Marxist record is awful."[8]

C. The Marxist critique, hermeneutic, and so-called exegesis of Scripture, I believe, are ultimately incompatible with United Methodism's commitment to revealed religion and must lead inevitably to a materialistic understanding of life and reality. I regard liberation theology's acceptance of the Marxist analysis of class struggle as a by-product of capitalistic society, together with the proposed Marxist solutions, as being distortions of the Christian gospel. In my judgment, grass-roots United Methodism in the United States of the 1980s will *never* endorse this perspective and will continue to be ruptured by its promulgation.*

5. Capitalism in today's United States urgently needs radical reform. It is being done to death in the house of its friends, and the unbridled abuses springing from individual and corporate greed have provided fertile soil in which to plant socialistic seeds. As long as the leaders of our nation continue to demonstrate calloused unconcern about the welfare of the hungry, the desperately poor, the unemployed, the homeless, those unable to provide necessary medical care for their families or themselves, the aged and the frightened, the

---

*I recognize, of course, that some of my episcopal colleagues serve in socialistic countries, and that their perspective on this matter may be radically different from my own. I respect them both as individuals and personal friends, and also the situations in which they make their witness and do their work.

principle of free enterprise will remain mortally imperiled in our land. Capitalism must become *open* to the little person and his or her brave efforts to secure a legitimate foothold in our economy. The products of our labor and managerial genius must be accessible to *all* our people. We must learn how to control profits, production, and distribution with some sense that the rights of society are paramount to the rights of individuals, as the great Kansas editor William Allen White reminded us fifty years ago,[9] yet leave individuals enough initiative and motivation to make for human progress.

I believe with all my heart in capitalism and free enterprise, but I believe in them as they ought to be and not as they are at this time. We need to ask ourselves John Cobb's blunt question, Can capitalism be Christian? We need also to be courageous enough as citizens of this country to alter present conditions until the answer is a clear affirmative. The difficulties may be formidable, but they can be overcome with intelligence and determination.

I know there are different expressions of the socialistic philosophy in the world. Some of them are far superior to others and some of them are employed constructively within basically capitalistic countries. However, I am convinced at this point that a free enterprise economy is able to promise in the end a fairer and more satisfactory life and better provision for the poor than other systems. I also believe that capitalism, like all other economic designs, must come constantly under the white light of Jesus Christ's judgment and that he cannot possibly be pleased with what he sees happening in the United States now.

6. I plead that the many good and wise Christian leaders of our church in this country now committed to liberation theology revise their own system, keeping their passionate determination to bring justice and liberty to the poor and oppressed, and that they be certain their revised system has no alliance with any philosophy that our presently troubled people can interpret as being either overtly or covertly a certain politico-economic system.

7. Some expressions of liberation theology, usually indirectly, have allowed the employment and blessing of violence if it is required to accomplish desired ends. Liberationists have crafted occasionally a curious doctrine that tolerates the interim absence of individual freedom in the long procession of revolutionary change. Thus they can bless Cuba, nearly overlook Afghanistan (and even the USSR), and find ways of rationalizing overt national repressions elsewhere behind the Iron Curtain. This careless alliance with violence and human slavery is simply not acceptable in a country where the memory of Martin Luther King, Jr., and Thomas Jefferson remains sacred. It would be far better for our own advocates of the liberation movement to assert clearly, as Moltmann seems to have done in Europe, that the people and leaders of our church here will never consider abandoning personal and political liberties, even to achieve a better economic system.

8. The insistences of liberation theology are *desperately* needed in our church today as far as they focus our attention upon the plight of the poor and the oppressed. However, to require a conscientious United Methodist Christian in this country to espouse, even passively, the overthrow of our present economic system and its replacement by another, in order to support programs of justice and righteousness for the unfortunate, is to place that individual in nearly an impossible position. Such action would damage the ultimate cause to which we are all committed and threaten a division of our church in a manner that is sure to diminish if not destroy completely its present will and ability to support its worldwide mission. One would hope devoutly that the many sincere proponents of liberation theology in our church would engage in realistic self-criticism at certain important points, undertake any revisionary procedure indicated, and make clear to the United Methodist people in the United States what their objectives really are, in order to bring unity to our church and its members in a manner that will conserve and invigorate our historic concern for redeeming systems as well as individuals.

Conclusion

Our United Methodist people are *hungry* for doctrine. They long for assurance that our church still believes and affirms the central truths of the Bible and Wesleyan religion. To receive this message from our pulpits, our Sunday school class lectures, and our local church study groups would dissipate a widespread disillusionment that has helped paralyze church growth.

We began this chapter with reference to Carlyle Marney's discussion of sin and grace. Added to these timeless religious ideas, for Wesleyan believers, must be justification by faith, sanctification, the eschatological affirmation of the final triumph of righteousness, prevailing prayer, and life everlasting. These are basic certainties that belong to our heritage.

But there is more. Our theology, in order to be communicable, must become doxology. It must be made to sing for our weary souls. It is reputed that William Ashley Sunday, the evangelist, said, "Theology is to religion what botany is to a rosebud." Without the science of botany, we would not have the loveliness of the rosebud, so, without the science of theology, we cannot have the power of religion. *But it is the strong, transforming power of religion which, in the end, we seek.*

A New York newspaper reporter ran out of his apartment on his way to the subway. As he went down the stairs he saw a lilac blossom lying on one of the steps. He stopped to pick it up, noticing that it still had a lingering fragrance about it. As he stood there and studied that lilac blossom, this Manhattan reporter suddenly remembered that beyond New York City it was spring in the country. Green things were growing and blooming in the fields. There was a blue mist on the mountains, and there were flowers everywhere. Holding that lilac blossom, he remembered a world that he had forgotten.

There is a spiritual world beyond the world we know. A little girl was asked in class one day to write down the things she thought most beautiful. This was her list: a thrush singing, snow falling, the reflection of street lights on the water, red velvet, the moon in the clouds. Our relationship with the Savior ought to have a beauty beyond the beauty of such things. It ought to have joy and ecstasy, the incredible kind of ecstasy that grips the soul of a person who has been saved from sin and knows that he or she is a child of God. E. Stanley Jones put it in his own vivid way: "I felt as though I had swallowed sunshine." In a day of religious sophistication, in a church which has properly emphasized the intellectual and the rational, I dare to lift a plea that we shall seek to recover a Christian's simple original rapture over Jesus Christ.

Thus our theology indeed will become doxology, and the church we love will be infused with new life.

CHAPTER FIVE

On Being Heralds of God

"Please send us a better preacher!"

How many times have I heard this earnest plea from Pastor-Parish Committees while I have been in the episcopal office! Sometimes the evaluation of the present preacher is woefully wrong: he or she *is* a good preacher, but for some reason the committee simply has not recognized it. However, more often than we wish, the committee is justified in its pleas.

I remember a number of years ago hearing Bishop John Owen Smith talk about an important church in the Atlanta Area. He said, "We've had good men for thirty years; now we need a *voice!*"

The American United Methodist pulpit constitutes one of the most influential forums in this nation. If we round off our total membership at nine million (persistent annual losses, before long, may make this an accurate or even an exaggerated figure), and if only 25 percent of these United Methodists are in church on a given Sunday, there are still 2,250,000 of our people exposed to the preaching of the Word of God each week. This does not take into account visitors, and of course it does not include different denominations and those in their sanctuaries. Although other parts of worship are of vast importance in mediating the miracle of Christian experience to a congregation, it is still true, particularly in the Protestant tradition, that the preaching event remains central. Therefore, we have an inescapable obligation to give continuing attention to its quality and effectiveness.

A First Word About Good Preaching

I have never found churches dead or Christian people discouraged and disillusioned where there is an exciting proclamation of the gospel from the pulpit. I have found too many present-day ministers either persuaded that preaching has lost its place in the church today, or unwilling themselves to pay the exacting price demanded of the individual who will become, in very fact, God's effective messenger on Sunday morning. Preaching is both a passion and a craft, and if a man or a woman is deficient at either point, that person does not accomplish a full ministry and the church to which he or she is assigned is deprived of its largest opportunity. The great battlefields upon which the war for social ideals and human liberty is waged are the battlefields of the human mind and spirit, and the preacher is foremost among the warriors. Can you preach? When you stand behind the sacred desk, does a mantle from heaven fall upon you?

Evangelist Gipsy Smith once told about a young minister who came to him for help in getting a church. The Gipsy posed an embarrassing question, "Can you preach?" The young man replied with humility, "I guess I wouldn't set the Thames on fire." "No," Mr. Smith said, "I suppose not. But if I threw you in, would you make it fizz?" This is my question to you and to myself, my brother and sister preachers.

At a Council of Bishops meeting, I heard about a Catholic priest and a rabbi playing golf together. At one hole, each had a difficult putt to make. The priest crossed himself and made his putt beautifully. The rabbi looked on in amazement, then said, "Father, would you mind if I crossed myself?" "No," replied the priest, "but it won't do you any good." "Why?" asked the rabbi. "Because you can't putt," replied the priest.

We have all known ministers who would never make the Thames fizz, who really can't preach. Fortunately, many of these possess compensating skills and abilities and are able to perform meaningful ministry, but how much better would be their contribution to the Kingdom if they could at least improve their homiletical work!

I have a simple conviction, hammered out on the anvil of my own experience: *any* minister can be a *better* preacher than he or she now is if that person is willing to pay the price in study, preparation, and prayer.

Harry Emerson Fosdick, writing in the July 1928 issue of

Harper's Magazine, said a basic thing in a manner that the passing years have never made obsolete: "Preaching is wrestling with individuals over questions of life and death, and until that idea of it commands a preacher's mind and method, eloquence will avail him little and theology not at all."

I suggest *six* prerequisites to effective preaching in pulpits large or small:

1. A conviction that preaching is important and can be effective
2. A personal knowledge of the living God and his gospel
3. Love for human beings, even the unlovable
4. Hard, grueling work
5. A terrible, frightening sense of urgency
6. Prevailing prayer

The late great Yale historian, Kenneth Scott Latourette, one of the authentic Christian saints of the twentieth century, used to speak of the manner in which God "sent His whisper" through him.[1] This sums up, for me at least, much of the thrilling awareness that overflows my soul when I step into a pulpit, and I am confident that a multitude of dedicated ministers in United Methodism would have the same sensitive response to Latourette's poetic words. I suppose I am pleading for a *recovery of a sense of the Lord's presence* among those of us who are ordained, for I believe that any improvement in the spiritual health of the church and its ministry has to begin with people like you and me. We must know the living God in the freshness of a new experience and assurance before we possess the fundamental credentials for good preaching. Leslie Weatherhead said in his book *Time for God:*

> When that strange, awesome sense of the numinous *does* fall upon the spirit, it is far more compelling and convincing about the reality of God's existence than are any intellectual arguments, valuable though these may be. It is as though one glimpsed on a Swiss holiday, for only a few moments, the shining, snow-clad peaks. Days of rain and mist may follow and the weather make the view as depressing as Bloomsbury in a November fog. But *one knows the peaks are there.*[2]

May God help this indispensable *inner certainty* to come to us again and afresh, and then help us share it excitingly from our pulpits! George Ade, the famous humorist, said one time, "The music teacher came twice each week to bridge the awful gap between Dorothy and Chopin!" So the whole preaching event is designed to be a vehicle through which the Spirit of God may bridge a wider gap between the "natural" person and the "spiritual" person.

If the content of our faith is flimsy and unsure, then we have little to preach, and it is mockery to ask the Holy Spirit to bless our shallow homilies. If we allow ourselves to be lured away from safe harbors by every new and novel wind of doctrine, then surely we are unfit to serve as spiritual guides for others. To preach in this age calls for discriminating and discerning knowledgeableness: the will to grasp the meaning of current theological thought and to comprehend what the consequences of such thought may prove to be. It means sorting out a little wheat from a lot of chaff in today's funny-looking theological granary and being willing to rephrase the church's gospel and restyle its strategy without abandoning its message or compromising its mission. To preach today means constructing with persistent sensitivity an image of the minister that can survive the ruthless scrutiny of a new and cynical age, an image based upon impeccable integrity instead of superficial piety, on candid awareness rather than what someone has called naïve "nincompoopery," on sureness of God instead of clever intellectual gymnastics. The minister who needlessly violates hospital visiting regulations, who invades the family rather than visits it, who feels an audible prayer coming on at some terribly inappropriate moment, who asks for a discount or hints for poundings, who faces daily tasks with a grotesque pomposity which is little more than ordained hyprocrisy, who tries with conspicuous indirection to inflate his or her salary, who has the flagrant dishonesty to parade personal peeves across the sacred terrain of a pulpit and under the banner of a biblical text is *anathema*, and he or she is one eloquent reason why the church perishes for want of renewal in our time!

If all of this sounds harsh, I am simply pleading that we who break the bread of life shall become willing to pay the *terrible* price involved in being better preachers than we have ever been before! Then our churches will be filled to overflowing with hungry people, then the Holy Spirit will visit our preaching with redeeming power, then will

> Heaven comes down our souls to greet,
> And glory crowns the mercy seat.*

I have been speaking somewhat in generalities; let me approach the matter of preaching now under certain *specific* topics.

The Content of Preaching

When Clarence Edward Macartney lay dying at the old family home in Beaver Falls, Pennsylvania, his preacher brother, who was attending him during his final illness, left one Sunday morning to preach a sermon at the local Presbyterian church. As he departed, he asked his sick brother if he had any advice about the sermon. "Put all the Bible you can in it," replied the great Pittsburgh preacher. That is still good counsel. Often the Word becomes its own message. The people will remember Scripture if they forget everything else (or if there is nothing else *worth* remembering).

A substantial portion of sound doctrine should also be presented clearly, comprehensibly, and palatably. If you think it cannot be done, you should read the stirring sermons and prayers given by Karl Barth over a period of years to the inmates of the prison at Basel, Switzerland. At times he sounds like an old-fashioned Methodist circuit rider, and his illustrations range from an allusion to the artist Holbein to an almost nostalgic recollection of his experience with cod-liver oil as a child![3] Or you should talk to someone who attended the Fraumünsterkirche, Zurich's fifteenth-century cathedral where Emil Brunner Sunday after Sunday proclaimed with eloquent persuasiveness his profound dogmatics in such simple, moving language that his townspeople said when he

---

*Hugh Stowell, "From Every Stormy Wind That Blows."

spoke, Fraumünster was a place you could send your housemaid.[4] Or again, you should buy and read Reinhold Niebuhr's sermons edited and published after his death by his wife, which are stunning examples of the prophetic and clear use of difficult passages of Scripture to communicate exciting insights into Christian truth.[5]

Never can my wife and I forget an experience in the fall of 1943 when we heard Dr. Niebuhr lecture. We saw then what since much reading has only served to document, namely that his vast and far-reaching social concern was set permanently in a deeply religious context. His words were clear, often moving, but most of his gesturing and many of his inflections were accomplished by those piercing, probing eyes! I remember one sentence in his lecture: "When Paul speaks of the peace that surpasses understanding, he means it is such because it is a peace that has pain in it." In 1959 Niebuhr said, "I am a preacher and I like to preach."

The sermons of Barth, Brunner, and Niebuhr bristle with deep doctrinal truth, far more thrillingly stated in their preaching than the average person would find in Barth's *Church Dogmatics* (which massive work actually sprang from the author's concern about proclaiming the Word), the several volumes of Brunner's *Dogmatik,* or Niebuhr's *Gifford Lectures.* Preaching is dramatically different from scholarly writing or lecturing! Nels Ferré,[6] in his posthumously published sermons, and the several sermon volumes by Scotland's great teacher-preacher James S. Stewart are additional examples of the marvelous way the masters have been able to set the great creedal affirmations of the Christian faith to the music and rhythm of popular idioms. I believe that any reasonably able, careful preacher can learn to do the same, perhaps to a lesser degree. It is God's truth as expressed in *historic* evangelical religion that nourishes the human spirit and life; and this truth, albeit complex and complicated in its scholarly or academic form, can be communicated simply enough so that wayfaring men "and fools shall not err therein" (Isa. 35:8).

A preacher must not be afraid to deal with the *great* theological ideas in the Christian message. Some are, and one is easily reminded of Joseph Conrad's scathing judgment on

Henry James: "He was the hippopotamus chasing a pea." So it is with preaching when it insists on dealing with trivia!

One of my fondest recollections of the late Henry Burton Trimble is a series of sermons he preached in a church I served during my early ministry in the Holston Conference. One sermon was on the subject "God"; another was on "Redemption"; still another was on "Eternity." To a fledgling homiletician this was pure, unmitigated audacity! But he was at his glorious best in those three sermons. They were like Matterhorns bathed in the crystal clear light of beautiful mornings! It takes a lot of study, a lot of living, and a lot of praying to marshal the courage necessary to confront your congregation with the massive theological propositions of our holy faith and to do it in a way that illuminates instead of darkens their glory. But this is genuine teaching-preaching, the kind that nourishes both the spirit and the mind, and the kind that endures.

Someone said that Robert Louis Stevenson "died with a thousand stories in his heart." I once heard Professor Stewart stop in the middle of an address and say, "If I should live two lifetimes, I could not preach all the sermons that are in my soul!"

No preacher has a right to waste the precious moments given to him or her on Sunday morning by serving up to spiritually famished worshipers a mess of religious twaddle! And, I venture to add, no preacher should be convinced that an adequate job of proclaiming the gospel of Jesus Christ can be accomplished with a *ten- or twelve-minute* sermon! The prominence of a message with content in the Protestant tradition was never achieved by such truncated presentations. I know many churches, some in my own conference, where this kind of abbreviated pulpit utterance is in vogue. I know some preachers who practice it, but I still recommend with all the urgency of my soul a *twenty- or twenty-five-minute* sermon!

Preaching itself is quite unlike any other form of public address, both in its nature and its objectives. Some ministers apparently do not comprehend this fact readily. A true sermon is not a book review, a travelogue, a commentary on current news, a church program commercial, or a vehemently delivered apologetic for something the preacher has said or done which probably ought not to have been said or done.

In his Lyman Beecher Lectures a dozen years ago, David H. C. Read reminded us that preaching is not "the attempt to sow religious ideas," nor is it "a moral prod to the conscience," nor yet "an effort to provide mild therapy for the victims of tensions and strain."[7]

T. R. Glover put the expectations of parishioners quite clearly when he said, "I won't give tuppence for the man who goes into the pulpit to tell me what my duty is, but I'll give all for the man who goes into the pulpit to tell me whence my help comes!"

Preaching is, according to the late Harold Cooke Phillips, "bearing witness to the truth."[8] All of us who have ever attempted it, no matter what our favorite definition of the act is, are aware that preaching involves intelligent and responsible dealing with God's Word in the biblical message under a power quite beyond our human skill and understanding. This means uncompromisingly hard work. It means competency in exegesis and exposition, areas of homiletical education sorely neglected in my student generation. Parenthetically, a major step toward improving pulpit performance would be taken if all of our United Methodist seminaries would include in their curricula relevant courses on preaching taught by exciting preacher-professors, and then *require* every ministerial student to take some of them!

An irresistible compulsion lies upon the preacher to communicate the message, as Jeremiah understood well when he said: "There is in my heart as it were a burning fire shut up in my bones, and I am weary with holding it in, and I cannot" (Jer. 20:9). True preaching, even after the most careful preparation has been made, is still an event that at some point and in some manner is taken beyond the control of the preacher.

The Craft of Preaching

Phillips Brooks, in his Lyman Beecher Lectures, gave his famous definition of preaching as the presentation of truth through personality. This has to mean *your personality or mine*.

There are rules, to be sure. One of the most important is a clear outline. Another is impeccably correct grammar (our minds ought to be branded with this one!). A third is vivid, but never purple, language. A fourth is a carefully cultivated, well-modulated voice as far removed from the stentorian tones of the stereotyped preacher as the East is from the West! A fifth is the deliberate and consistent elimination of sexist language in all human allusions. Many will disagree with me when I say that I choose to retain the masculine references to God and the Holy Spirit. I give my personal reasons for this position elsewhere in these pages and respect the right of others to hold a different conviction. A final rule would be a transparent sincerity and an impelling urgency able instantly to convey the excitement and glory of the preacher's own personal faith to his or her listeners. Someone who heard James Stewart preach in Charlotte, North Carolina, said afterward, "I was embarrassed by the *immensity* of his belief."

These are basic guidelines that any effective preacher must master. Having learned them and learned them well, the good preacher goes on from there. The fresh new wine of his or her message may burst old wineskins. Urgent eagerness to communicate the wonder of the Christian message may cause the preacher to take liberties never prescribed or permitted by rules.

Olin Downes, music critic for a great newspaper, heard the master pianist Horowitz perform a Tchaikovsky concerto on two different occasions twenty-five years apart. Describing his second experience, Downes recalled that the first time Horowitz played the concerto it was meticulously correct with every note accorded proper attention and the result exquisitely precise and accurate. But the second time, a quarter of a century later, Downes recorded that Horowitz surged beyond the technical accuracy and precision of his earlier performance and became, in the critic's words, "gigantic, unpolished, imprudent, overwhelming!"

This reminds me of the first time I heard Dr. Stewart preach. I had read his great books of sermons and knew that they were pure, perfect literature in themselves. His writing was incredibly symmetrical and eloquent. I expected his preaching to be the same, with every *i* dotted and every *t* crossed, but I was in for a startling experience. The great Scotsman became so enthralled with his message, so recklessly eager to make its meaning and challenge clear to those of us listening that he suddenly began to pound the pulpit like an old-time country preacher. He left sentences trailing off in mid-air, unfinished, as he rushed on to others that clamored to be spoken. The gospel he was proclaiming consumed him, and the fires in his own soul set ours aflame. This is preaching, but it can only happen when a careful craftsman has mastered all the rules and been mastered by them, so that his preacher's soul may safely take flight and the winds of the Spirit catch and carry the gospel truth into the hearts of worshipers. There are many ways to describe this sacred process that transforms a Christian pulpit into a place of mystical spiritual power, but Bishop Roy H. Short used to put it simply when he said that such a preacher had *"unction"*!

The craft of preaching demands something else before any of the above can take place. It requires disciplined toil and dedicated study. Harry Emerson Fosdick is reputed to have said that for every minute he was on his feet preaching one solid hour of careful study had gone into preparation. Some preachers can use a manuscript with great effectiveness (Phillips Brooks and Peter Marshall were examples), and some cannot. A bishop hears many churches complain because preachers read their sermons. Perhaps, on the whole, it is better to master a manuscript to the point where it does not require reading; but let it be firmly stated that every sermon should have its manuscript whether it is carried into the pulpit or not. The precision and vigor of careful wording cannot be achieved otherwise, nor can clarity and appropriate brevity.

A recent book by Richard Eslinger[9] offers a helpful summary of new homiletic approaches. I regret that a contemporary reinterpretation of classical preaching designs (still amazingly effective in many situations) is not more vigorously pursued by some of the able new authors in this field.

Many of our church problems would be solved if we could overcome the mental as well as physical laziness that grips some preachers. Preaching is poor usually because there has not been adequate preparation for the pulpit. Bishop Hughes once said to a class of young preachers coming into full connection, "The most dangerous thing that can ever happen to you is for you to discover that you are able to speak extemporaneously!"

Delivery is important and different today. The dialogical approach has replaced the hortatory, perhaps largely because of the growing influence wielded by television's effective communicators such as Cronkite, Rather, and Donahue. It has been difficult for me to learn this new approach, but if I were a young preacher I would do it or die. Language is important too and needs to employ contemporary and familiar idioms. Illustrations should reflect current knowledge and experience, and often seem most effective when they are drawn *discreetly* from life situations. This is not to say that allusions to the classics are passé, or that an occasional telling quotation will not strengthen pulpit argument. Rather it is to insist that preachers must always be controlled by the desire to get their message over to the people in a way they can understand and in a form they can take home with them for reference throughout a new week.

New approaches to preaching are constantly in the process of development. An exciting one of these is described by Eugene L. Lowry in his book entitled *Doing Time in the Pulpit*.[10] He suggests that the modern sermon should employ a narrative hermeneutic and be imaged as a story. In an earlier book Edmund A. Steimle, Morris J. Niedenthal, and Charles L. Rice, from three different seminaries, had explored a similar approach, lifting up the idea of preaching as storytelling and the preacher as raconteur.[11*] When I first read Frederick Buechner, I discovered that he believes in a similar way of communicating the gospel.[12] Why not? We continue to diminish the church's chances in a new and vastly changed day of human history if we insist on espousing the same old methods instead of being bold enough to try something fresh. After all, our message is the important thing.

In recent years particularly, United Methodism has benefited from the unique and thrilling characteristics of Black preaching. Every white preacher ought to read some of the excellent books written on this subject and learn also from intentional exposure to the actual preaching event in Black churches. Many of our predominately white congregations, I am persuaded, would be receptive of their ministers' reproduction of some of Black preaching's extraordinary qualities. When we have worshiped with Black people, my wife says, "I feel as though I have been to church today!"

The traditional Black church will not tolerate easily a preacher who cannot communicate. Thomas Carlyle once said, "I wish that speaking man would find the point again, for there's need of him yet." The Black preacher usually knows how to find the point and how to share it with his or her hearers. Too, the typical Black congregation employs *emotion* (but rarely emotionalism) freely and richly in developing the experience of worship. Black people, understandably because of their years of suffering and persistent dreaming of a better day, have sought and found in church attendance, and particularly in the sermon, sources of help and strength for living between Sundays. One of the greatest sermons I ever heard was preached by Bishop Alexander P. Shaw in the mid-1950s. It was entitled "Sometimes I Feel Like a Motherless Child." I couldn't have equaled it in a hundred years!

Preparing the Preacher

An inveterate liberal friend of mine went voluntarily to hear an adamant fundamentalist preach. I asked him why. A very sensitive man, he replied with tears in his eyes, "Do you know the personal integrity of this preacher? Do you know the tragedy he has overcome in his own life? No matter that he is a fundamentalist, I would go anywhere to hear him tell me about God."

An indispensable credential for any preacher is still the moral and religious quality of his or her life. Perhaps no words in recent decades have been more openly despised in theological circles than "pietism" and "moralism," and to some extent understandably, for honest people have seen in them violent misuse of the preaching event and a verbal microcosm of the age-old pharisaism and hypocrisy that have so often been grave embarrassments to the Christian community. However, the pity is that modern rejection of these terms has sometimes been extended mistakenly to imply a tragic depreciation of the whole idea of ethical quality and personal integrity in an individual's life.

Cleanness of thinking, speaking, and living is in some quarters no longer regarded as an unmistakable hallmark of Christian faith. Indeed, we passed through a period when filthy speech, unconventional morals, and sometimes loosely rationalized acts of violence or near-violence were justified by religious argument and advocated by stellar names in the religious community. But we can never get away from the simple, devastating fact that the experience of religion has to make a *qualitative* difference in a person's life and relationships. To deny this is to surrender to the largest of all illusions. One cannot remember the teachings of Augustine, Anselm, Calvin, or Wesley, much less the troublesome New Testament witness to the pristine purity and devotional discipline of Jesus, without realizing that the severing of personal piety from theological reflection is, put mildly, a dangerous development. The plain fact is that sermons, through the centuries, have had their greatest power when they have been preached by *good* men and women, people whose own lives quietly but surely mirrored the gospel of which they spoke.

Do you remember Charles Dickens' comment about one of his characters, "He was fuller of virtuous precepts than a copy book, but like a guide post that pointed the way but never went himself"? Even Nietzsche took up the cry with the words, "These Christians must show me they are redeemed, before I will believe in their Redeemer!" And Professor John Knox, in an address I heard him give years ago, said, "When I think of men in the ministry who have helped me most, *I think not of the gifted but of the good.*"

In spite of philosophical and theological detours of recent years, some being largely responsible for the church's plight today, Archbishop Soderblom did not exaggerate when he said, "*Holiness* is the *great* word of religion; it is even more essential than the notion of God." We need desperately to lift the grand New Testament term "saint" out of the strange disrepute into which it has fallen in some quarters of the

Christian community. The pursuit of holiness, or the New Testament ideal of personal excellence, is not just a human enterprise; rather it is a clear prescription of the gospel, as these passages suggest: "This is the will of God, your *sanctification*" (I Thess. 4:3, italics added); "Even as he chose us in him before the foundation of the world, that we should be *holy* and *blameless* before him" (Eph. 1:4, italics added); "As God's chosen ones, *holy* and *beloved*" (Col. 3:12a, italics added).

What I have been speaking of does not come to any minister overnight. It is a cumulative result deriving from a clear relationship with God and a determined adherence to the disciplined life-style of a biblical Christian. It is fundamental to effective preaching.

There is another aspect to the preparation of the preacher. It is more immediate. Dr. Buttrick used to say that he spent five days preparing his sermon, but the sixth day he prepared himself. The quiet clearing of the mind where extraneous or disturbing thoughts are concerned (not always possible, to be sure), a deliberate and private time of devotional exposure to Scripture, the saturation of one's soul in a fresh experience of prayer, perhaps a bracing walk in the brisk open air, a good night's sleep, and a time of renewed fellowship with loved ones—all of these can be important in getting a preacher ready to go behind the sacred desk on Sunday morning. There will be some times, to be sure, when such practices are impossible. Perhaps a person is sick, or has had to spend most of Saturday night with a bereaved family or an alcoholic, or perhaps an avalanche of personal problems has crushed the preacher's soul. God knows and understands these things, and he also knows the frightening regularity with which Sunday morning rolls around. These are the times when the Holy Spirit comes to our aid in special ways, and our appeal for his assistance under such conditions is entirely justifiable. To ask for his help under different circumstances, specifically when we have elected to fritter away precious hours that ought to have been used in study, is to insult him by expecting him to function as a labor-saving device!

The preparation of the preacher, long-term and immediate, is indispensable for effective preaching.

The Paradox and the Miracle

A final very imporant word needs to be said.

David H. C. Read declares, "When we think of preaching as *mystery,* we are restoring it to its proper place in the enduring life of the church."[13] The Apostle Paul in I Corinthians 1:21 says, "For since, in the wisdom of God, the world did not know God through wisdom, it pleased God through the folly of what we preach to save those who believe." A bit earlier (I Cor. 1:18) he had reminded us, "For the word of the cross is folly to those who are perishing, but to us who are being saved it is the power of God." There is something about preaching that will always defy human understanding and that can never be captured in class notes for a course in homiletics.

Perhaps the late D. T. Niles came closest to an explanation when he told the story of Piérre Maury leaping to his feet during meetings of the Central Committee of the World Council of Churches in Paris and crying out in the midst of discussions "This is a *saved* world!"[14] Victory is implicit in the gospel. The idea of *prolepsis* is an appropriate companion for the idea of *proclamation.* When you and I have done our humble best, after a thoroughgoing discipline of prayer and study, a miracle will occur. The late Helmut Thielicke summed it up:

> God will acknowledge you and He will not let His Word return to Him void. When it returns to you it will be freighted with the answers and the decisions of those who have heard it. And because God Himself is on the battlefield, there is no need for the presumptuous assumption that the right thoughts will occur to you at the right moment. God's own Spirit will enter into you and He Himself will confront men through your poor words. While you contend, Another will contend for you.[15]

Once, when I had preached, a friend, superintendent of schools in my home city, came down to the front of the church and handed me a slip of paper with three sentences written on it. I read them, and they became part of my life. "He stood *before* the cross and spoke; the people saw him, heard a voice but heeded not. He stood *beside* the cross and spoke, the people saw him and the cross, heard his voice, but heeded not.

He stood *behind* the cross and spoke; the people saw not the preacher, but the cross, heard the voice of Jesus, and were saved." I needed the message—and need it still.

Do you need this lesson too, my brother and sister preachers?

CHAPTER SIX

The "Glory of the Lighted Mind"*

I do not believe that the *merely church-related college* is likely to survive far beyond the passing of the present century. But I believe with all the fervor of my soul that the courageously committed *Christian* college has its surest and brightest days ahead of it—in spite of all its problems, particularly the ogre of spiraling educational costs and the new difficulty posed for philanthropy by a badly needed revision in American income tax law.

I think I know about most of the issues that intensify the United Methodist college administrator's perennial insomnia. Among these are the following:

1. The escalation in the costs which either parents or students must pay for four years of higher education in private institutions. I remember well an administrative council meeting at Emory and Henry College twenty-eight years ago when we spent an entire morning debating the proposed elevation of the package price for a student the next year; the figure was $1,000, including tuition, fees, room, and board!

2. The complicated difficulty of choosing a competent and dedicated Christian faculty when current laws place severe

---

*Line from John Masefield's poem "The Everlasting Mercy."

There are two important subjects with which this chapter does not deal, simply because it was necessary to limit its scope. The first is the campus ministry at our public colleges and universities. As a missional thrust of our church, it has such impressive significance as to merit separate treatment. The second is the university related to United Methodism (there are nine at this writing). Because of the substantive difference between a college and a university, the two cannot be addressed adequately together. However, it may be noted gratefully that most, if not all, of our United Methodist universities approach their stewardship of liberal education and moral values seriously.

restrictions on the nature and number of questions that can be asked during employment interviews.

3. The legal labyrinth of a day when acts of litigation are innumerable and often weird. A serious concomitant of this is the threat sometimes implicit in maintaining an open relationship to the church in institutional charters, operational bylaws, and even names, primarily because of lower court decisions about the connectional nature and responsibility of United Methodism still standing from the era of the Pacific Homes episode. All of this is complicated further by the growing difficulty and high cost of obtaining and retaining adequate liability insurance and coverage to protect directors and officers.

4. The possible reduction in charitable giving in the United States by as much as $13,000,000,000 annually as a result of tax reform—much of which loss is sure to impact private institutions of higher education. This will test the religious motivation of givers, since tax advantages may be lessened substantially. Editorial director Harold Evans, writing in the September 1, 1986, issue of *U.S. News & World Report,* affirmed his belief that "the heart of America . . . (will) be good" for the amounts required to permit eleemosynary institutions to continue their work. But the time of testing for our United Methodist colleges and universities will be grim, and the immediate impact of the problem could prove severe.

5. The overarching problem of dealing with today's pervading secularism, which one United Methodist college president recently declared is the most foreboding barrier confronting the Christian institution. A large part of this centers in the kind of students, even from United Methodist families, who are available today—frequently poorly grounded in academic fundamentals and often already exposed if not addicted to drugs, alcohol, sexual liberty, and practiced disinterest in the things of religion and the church. The maintenance of high campus conduct standards is made infinitely harder by this reality, although there are encouraging exceptions, both in the quality of students matriculating and in institutions still insisting courageously on Christian ideals in campus citizenship.

The "Glory of the Lighted Mind"—

A Brief History of a Relationship

That there is a significant reciprocal responsibility existing between many branches of the Christian Church and higher education is a condition growing out of the simple fact that education itself in modern times is largely a product of the direct and indirect influences of the church. In seasons of colorful academic gowns and hoods we may well recall that these were originally the costumes of learned monks. Perhaps no movement in the last five hundred years has given quite the impetus to education that came from the Protestant Reformation.

The origin of celebrated American colleges and universities further reinforces the fact about which I am speaking. In the little village of Branford, Connecticut, ten ministers of the gospel each set a few books on a table; this was the beginning of what is now Yale University. Harvard, Dartmouth, and Amherst were all children of the Congregationalists. William and Mary in Virginia and Columbia in New York were progeny of the Anglicans or Episcopalians. The list could be extended. By 1860 the churches of America had established 179 permanent colleges; and even the twenty-eight state or municipal institutions existing at that time were almost all headed by Christian ministers.

No wonder Alexis de Tocqueville, surveying life in America, wrote these words: "In the United States the influence of religion is not confined to the manners, but extends to the intelligence of the people."

The record of The United Methodist Church is remarkable in this arena of Christian mission. At the time these words are being written, we have 128 schools, colleges, universities, professional schools, and seminaries operating under the auspices of our denomination. No other religious communion except Roman Catholicism can approach this record.

Contemporary Anti-Intellectualism

It seems to me that we are moving posthaste into a largely unrecognized and unacknowledged era of anti-intellectualism in our own country and perhaps in Western civilization. The educational revolution is both sweeping and devastating. In much of our public school system today the element of substantive content in classroom teaching and the factor of disciplined demands on the student have vanished in a manner so total as to release on colleges and universities generations of young men and women who can neither read nor write with acceptable accuracy and have never been introduced at all to the skills of study and thought. The necessity for hard-pressed institutions to admit such young people, complicated by a fear of economically disastrous attrition and apprehension over costly litigation initiated by disgruntled students and parents, in many instances has caused the virtual collapse of even reasonable standards of quality and excellence. Dean Rosovsky of the Harvard faculty said a few years ago in a letter to his teachers, "The B.S. degree is becoming little more than a certificate of attendance."

What we have traditionally referred to as liberal education, or the liberal arts, may be in a state of terminal illness in our time—in spite of the modest encouragement afforded by certain recent reports. It has always insisted on exposure to the great books and concepts of the centuries, including the Bible and the ideas of Christianity. It glories in grappling with the hard questions of human existence and experience, the stubborn but intriguing "why" issues. It deliberately seeks to train the student to *think* and struggles to develop an ability to make value judgments. Most significantly, it offers the option of God and informed faith, an understanding of the place of the spiritual in the wholeness of life.

That America's love affair with higher education may have moved into its twilight is evidenced in other ways. The voracious appetite of our country's public for television productions of the intellectual level of the afternoon or evening soap operas, the popularity of "frothy," sex-saturated novels, and the dramatically lessened demand on the part of industry and business for the scholarly products of educational institutions are circumstances in point. The introduction of computer science, itself devised and designed by an elitist intelligentsia, has made it unnecessary to employ as many well-trained minds. Anyone seeking employment recently realizes that the specter of "overqualification" looms large on the horizon, meaning simply that the short-term monetary objectives motivating much of current business leadership make it unprofitable to become involved with anyone whose level of preparation is likely to require an escalation of wages or salary.

Of significance is the emergence in recent years of the community college and the technical schools, although in fairness it must be acknowledged that some of the former are now beginning to acquire higher academic standards and more complete curricula. However, the emphasis is definitely on teaching skills for earning a living rather than imparting knowledge for living a life. Three years ago Group Attitudes Corporation's survey showed that 86 percent of all adults rated preparation for a career to be the most important reason for attending college. Nearly half of all bachelor degrees are now given in strictly occupational fields such as engineering and business—double the percentage of eighteen years ago. Deliberate enrollment in the studies related to liberal arts has dropped to a low of 7 to 10 percent, while 70 percent of all first-year college students state frankly that they are attending institutions of higher learning in order to make more money. The temptation confronting the Christian college to alter its own curriculum in response to popular demand is a real one, and many in the wider Christian community have at least begun to capitulate to it. The problem is critical for the church, the nation, and human civilization itself—*far more critical than the average local church member knows, and often more serious than the Christian minister has stopped to realize.*

Two Important Implications

I am grateful for state-supported higher education and for many excellent members of its faculties and administrations. We never can function again without it or them, but I often pause to remember that the Christian college is *the conscience of all higher education,* the sentinel that watches over academic freedom and the guardian of the integrity of the human quest for knowledge and truth. It is immune to political pressures and the whims of state legislatures. The lesson of the German universities and their convenient silence over the Nazi peril teaches us well at this point, as Einstein pointed out years ago.

There is another and more serious implication of the problem with which we are dealing. I do not believe that the United States, or Western civilization itself can hope to survive in the years ahead without the influence and impact of the Christian college. In this country our entire system of jurisprudence is based on insights and teachings to be found in the Judeo-Christian tradition. The concept of responsible individual freedom protected by the state and the credit system, at the heart of our economic structure, are both based on the assumption that there are more good people than bad. If this ever ceases to be so, we could easily have a police state and be required to pay for everything we purchase in cash. The kind of life represented in the vision of the American Revolution, which we cherish now in this Republic, cannot survive unless its primary leadership has been educated in institutions sensitive to the reality of the sacred, institutions that build moral awareness and value response and provide exposure to the rich religious legacy of human culture and history. If there is a chance for the church of Jesus Christ to shape the politics and economy of this country into something more akin to the kingdom of God, that chance depends almost entirely on the availability of highly trained, deeply committed Christian leaders. Thus our stake in the future of the Christian college is enormous, even though only a slight consciousness of this exists in the average local church!

What Is a Christian College?

There are certain characteristics that identify the Christian college, sometimes present to some extent in any private or church-related institution but, as I view the matter, not necessarily in the same manner or with the same intensity of purpose. *In my opinion, it is necessary for a college of the church to cultivate these characteristics and perform their ministries before it has a right to expect the church to support it financially and otherwise.* The college's persistent failure to do this will result in a further blurring of the line of distinction between public and Christian institutions in the minds of ordinary laypeople in our denomination.

Let me deal now with some of these characteristics.

1. *The Christian college is still interested in the student as a person.* The primary glory of the little college has always been that the individual student mattered—supremely and utterly. The impersonal anonymity of the throng never invades the "pleasant green" of the small institution. This is dramatically significant in these days of wholesale education and the monstrous super-university. We shall, and perhaps must, have the great super-university always henceforth with us; this is guaranteed by the population and information explosions and by precise technical specializations. However, its very presence will cause thoughtful men and women once more to place premium value on the small liberal arts institution of high quality and uncompromised purpose—the college where students and faculty are still magnificently in touch.

The Christian campus exists for the sake of the students, and their academic trepidations, luckless romances, inbred laziness, vague and sometimes topsy-turvy moral values, apprehensions, vulgar rowdiness, and roseate idealism are all of vast concern and grave consequence to every member of the faculty and staff. There is small comfort in this realization—as a former college president well knows—but there is unending challenge and enormous satisfaction.

Many of today's students are in the volcanic center of an identity crisis induced at once by the weird confusion of the times and the collapse of conventional landmarks in character and personality. This is a familiar phenomenon of our era.

When Willy Loman, the tragic hero in Arthur Miller's *Death of a Salesman,* says, "I have a right to know who I am," he utters the tortured plea of many modern youth. Much later, as you will recall, when Willy's wife and son stand at Willy's grave, after all the mourners have left, Biff, the son, utters one of the most haunting lines in modern drama, "He never knew who he was."

If we could understand that modern young people fear that they will never discover who they are or what is the meaning of life, surely we would take a long step toward bridging the generation gap. The Christian knows that the only satisfying answer to this query is in the message of Jesus Christ, and this equips the Christian college uniquely to deal effectively wherever the identity crisis presents itself.

There was a time, in another century, when colleges imposed what today would seem utterly unreasonable demands and restrictions upon students. For example, I once found a copy of the 1874 Emory and Henry catalog and discovered this language in its introductory paragraphs:

> Students are expected to attend all classes without fail. Any absence must be for an excellent reason. *Thanksgiving and Christmas are no reasons at all.*

Even more startling were the provisions articulated forty years earlier in the Mount Holyoke catalog:

> No young lady shall become a member of Mount Holyoke Seminary who cannot kindle a fire, mash potatoes, repeat the multiplication tables, and at least two-thirds of the Shorter Catechism.
>
> Every member of the school shall walk a mile a day unless a freshet, earthquake or some other calamity prevent.
>
> No young lady shall devote more than an hour a day to miscellaneous reading. No lady is expected to have gentlemen acquaintances unless they are returned missionaries, or agents of benevolent societies.

The times indeed have changed! But even infinitely lighter contemporary campus rules, particularly those likely to be found in a Christian college, often cramp the style of modern young people. When this problem is complicated by others, including difficult courses, failed examinations, and academic probation of one type or another, many students suffer terribly and simply must have help.

At this point the Christian college is in a position to render what is often unique service. Everyone on campus is involved, largely because everyone is accessible—the president, the deans, faculty members, chaplain, housemothers, sometimes even the maintenance crew, and the kitchen help. I remember, when I was a college president, lending a student $5 to finance a very important date (those were the days when candlelight dinners were cheap!). There was a professor on my faculty who confessed to me that he and his wife typed a term paper for one of his students because the student's typewriter broke down and the teacher for whom the term paper was being written had specified that it must be submitted in typed form.

Thinking back over eight years on a campus, I recall attempted suicides stopped, abrupt terminations of education prevented by quiet reasoning, shattered faith (due to some bereavement or disaster) restored, unwise romances discontinued (and wiser ones encouraged), hope given back when despair had taken it away, patient counsel offered about a thousand different issues, all because *an individual student mattered supremely* and there was someone there to do something about it! I even remember two students who had failed chemistry telling me how much the laboratory instructor had meant to them throughout their unfortunate experience. "If it hadn't been for Mr. Wheeler," one of them said, "we wouldn't even have made an F!"

Mostly it was the teachers who helped, for a teacher is not simply one who lectures and gives examinations; *a teacher lights up dark places.* John Erskine may have been right when he said, "A good teacher is so rare that the rumor of him spreads like a scandal." However, this observation would often apply far less on the campus of a Christian college than elsewhere. I doubt if there is any church college anywhere that hasn't been known for at least a few extraordinary and magnificent teachers, remarkable scholars who had a warm, compassionate concern for young men and women—all dramatically disproportionate to the size of their paychecks!

None of us can express sufficient gratitude to the professional teachers of United Methodism, not forgetting those who engage in theological pioneering and research scholarship. Theirs is a ministry demanding massive preparation, dogged commitment, and indefatigable toil—often far away from arenas of glory! They are one of the church's greatest gifts to its youth and one of its precious legacies to civilization.

I know from experience as a parent that the Christian college has something very special to offer its students in the way of understanding, support, and the kind of love that supplies light in the midst of dreadful darkness.

Our religion teaches us that every person, even the sinner, the mixed-up rebel, and the stupid fool, is of infinite worth—one for whom the Son of God died. Perhaps the *first* task of the Christian college is to express that philosophy in policy and deed.

2. *The Christian college still emphasizes the fundamentals.* The president of the New York Times Foundation, in a recent address, stated that an estimated 13 percent of all high school graduates today are *functional illiterates.* He went on to declare that textbook publishers are now revising high school texts to a *sixth-grade level of comprehension.* There are preachers in our pulpits, large and small, and sometimes in print as well, who make more basic errors in the use of English grammar than Dwight Lyman Moody, America's greatest evangelist who had only a fifth-grade education, ever did.

The entire task of teaching fundamentals in a way that is consonant with today's complex culture has been complicated beyond all measure by the *mass* of materials that compose the content of learning today. It is a staggering fact that the fund of available knowledge now *doubles every ten years.*

The requirements for the kind of basic education historically related to civilized learning may not have changed a great deal. When Woodrow Wilson was president of Princeton University, he reminded us that there are *four* characteristics of an educated person. An educated person must know: (1) the general history of the world, (2) the history of human ideas, (3) one of the sciences, and (4) one language, preferably, said Mr. Wilson, his own! The overall object of the classical liberal education has been to produce a well-rounded student perhaps capable, as Professor William James said many years ago, of recognizing a good person when he sees one. Robert Frost put it another way: "What we do in college is to get over our little-mindedness."

An adequate knowledge of the fundamentals is the foundation upon which civilization itself rests from generation to generation. The technical or vocational emphases in the educational process, important as they are in days like these, can never replace the academic emphases. There must be, at any cost, faculty members who are equipped to insist on this and who practice the kind of winsome pedagogy that can inspire in students a consuming desire to master basics.

3. *The Christian college still strives to teach a student to think.* It is never the plethora of facts and statistics one is required to absorb in the journey through college or university that matter most. It is the steady, quiet cultivation of a student's intellect in mastering that performance which, more than any other, sets God's higher creation apart from his lower creation, the art of *thinking*. Professor Ebling was right when he declared, "The faith that is afraid to think is unbelief in the mask of piety."

The Christian college majors in cultivating the ability to think. Let me suggest three ways in which this happens.

First, there is the development of the *habit of inquiry*. Plato said long ago, "The mark of a philosopher is wonder." James Watt wondered about a kettle, Newton about an apple, Archimedes about a bath.

Someone has suggested that the life of the mind is basically curiosity overcoming inertia.

Second, there is the development of the *power of discernment*. This is learning to evaluate, to choose, to refine the ability involved in rational judgment. The teacher at his or her best *must* be *a troubler of waters,* but must never leave the student to navigate those troubled waters alone. The Christian college majors in this kind of guidance, remembering the warning of the distinguished historian Carl Becher: "A genuinely *detached* mind would lie among the facts of history like unmagnetized steel among iron filings, with no synthesis ever resulting."

Third, there is the development of what Alfred North

Whitehead called *"the habitual vision of greatness."* Such images of greatness confront the student in history, in exposure to the great ideas of philosophy, in literature, in a knowledge of the Bible, and in the exciting narrative of scientific discovery. The student must follow the heroic exploits of the human mind as it has gone again and again into the dim unknown to return with reports of a promised land.

Purely utilitarian education can teach the human mind how to function technically, mechanically, but it can never instruct it in the finely tempered skills of rational thought. In the end, the very principles of human freedom, justice, and survival depend on the ability of educated men and women to think, to evaluate, to make choices, to structure priorities. This is the business that the Christian college is forever dedicated to accomplish.

4. *The Christian college still trains for responsible citizenship and church membership.* Years ago I heard President Landrum Bolling of Earlham College illustrate the importance of the proper relation of Christian faith and learning by telling of visiting a beautiful home in the Bavarian Alps. The rooms were furnished in exquisite taste. Great art hung on the walls. The finest books lined the shelves of the library. The hi-fidelity record collection contained the world's most magnificent music. The home was that of Heinrich Himmler, ruthless exponent of racism and terrorism in World War II Germany. The memory of the hideous tragedy of Nazism is not too dim for us to glean the lesson of that allusion.

The young person who moves out of the cloistered halls of academe to take his or her place in the professions, business, industry, or government must not only be equipped with facts but must also be able to see and use these facts within the context of moral and ethical sensibility. To put it bluntly, we must continue to depend on Christian colleges and universities to prepare young people for responsible citizenship in an hour of apocalyptic peril when the rumblings of nuclear Armageddons are creating terrifying noises throughout the earth. The kind of citizenship taught on the campus of the Christian college, we can be sure, will never itself cause a person to become part of what President Eisenhower referred to as a military-industrial complex ready to plunge the world into war for monetary profit. A citizen of Paris, asked what he did in the French Revolution, replied, "I survived!" To accomplish only this for our generation by offering responsible leadership in the maintenance of peace among the nations and in the ultimate dismantling of nuclear weapons of war would in itself justify every dollar that has ever been spent on the Christian colleges of this land!

These colleges also train their students to be worthy church members. Ernest Cadman Colwell, sometime interim president of the University of Chicago and dean of its divinity school, child of a Methodist parsonage and great New Testament scholar, once made a statement that I have never been able to forget: "If I must choose between keeping the university and letting the church go and keeping the church and letting the university go, I will choose to keep the church and let the university go, because the church would have the intelligence to build the university again." What a declaration! What an elevated concept of the church! It is this quality of appreciation for the church which the Christian college always attempts to inculcate in its students.

Some time ago in Clearwater, Florida, a young couple said to me as we discussed their alma mater, a distinguished Christian institution in our United Methodist family: "It was DePauw University which taught us both that our highest task in life is to serve and strengthen the church of Jesus Christ. It was also DePauw that made us understand what courage the right kind of citizenship demands in these days."

5. *The Christian college still exposes students to the claims of the Lord Jesus Christ.* It never forces a student to accept God. It never crams religion down his or her throat, but it always remembers former Harvard President Nathan Pusey's shining sentence: "The objective of education is not a mere knowledge of values but a commitment to them."

Thirty-one years ago, when I was inaugurated as president of Emory and Henry College, I made this statement:

The old dichotomy between the culture of the mind and the conversion of the soul must be destroyed. The relevance of God and the redemptive process centering in Jesus Christ and His Person and work to the entire educational experience must be acknowledged with a candor and enthusiasm reminiscent of the great religious awakenings of the 18th and 19th centuries.

I have not changed my mind today. I believe with all my heart and soul that the intentionally Christian institution of higher learning, honest enough not to be ashamed of the gospel and bold enough to demand quality performance in the classroom, will have a ready-made constituency of support among thoughtful people in the Christian community in spite of such factors as spiraling costs and diminishing student enrollment. The Christian college exposes young men and women to the best possible presentation of the claims of Jesus Christ. This comes in many different ways, but perhaps most often through dedicated faculty members.

The late Professor Leroy Loemker was the greatest teacher I ever had—and the hardest. An authority on the German philosopher and mathematician Leibniz, he was the long-time dean of graduate studies at Emory University and (in the old days) a local elder in The Methodist Church. To a young professional student, struggling to master the formidable vocabulary of philosophy, his brilliance was mesmerizing, and the profundity of his thought revealed so articulately in his classroom lectures was nearly shattering. I shall never forget what he wrote on a book report that I submitted to him in the early days of our relationship: "You can do better than this, Earl, at least I *hope* so!" He was constantly probing into the minds and lives of the young theologues sitting in his classroom to determine the extent of their motivation, the depth of their commitment, and the quality of their spiritual integrity. With gentle but penetrating courtesy he made us realize what an awesome thing it is to be called to preach the gospel, and then he sent us back to our desks and our knees to search our own souls about the authenticity of our Christian experience.

The genuinely Christian institution is always engaged in a reasonable and academically acceptable effort to encourage fundamental commitments to Christian values and to Jesus Christ himself. Its students will always have a better than ordinary opportunity to emerge from four years of study not only as solidly educated individuals but also as persons captivated by New Testament Christianity.

It would not be appropriate for other types of educational institutions to entertain or implement such a magnificent obsession.

Recommendations

I have mentioned certain problems confronting those who administer Christian colleges in United Methodism today and sketched briefly the history of religion's relation to higher education in this country. I have spoken of the ultimate importance of the committed Christian college and attempted to describe five of its unique functions. I come now to a point where I should like to venture certain recommendations. My only competence for this attempt is the eight years of experience that I had as a Christian college president, augmented more recently by a continuing effort to keep abreast of developments in this complex arena.

1. United Methodism *must* make a solid decision to stay in the business of institutional higher education, even at the cost of investing more money than it ever meant to invest in its Christian colleges! The kind of Christianity in which we believe cannot survive otherwise.

2. It has an obligation to demand of the schools it supports an honest effort to achieve both *academic excellence* and a thrillingly *unique Christian identity*.

3. It should begin an intensive campaign to educate local churches about the importance of the Christian college and its bearing on the kind of life we cherish for the United States and the world.

4. The liberal arts principle, in the light of a radically changing society, should be scrutinized carefully and modified appropriately if it is to function in the years ahead. The classical concepts of Cardinal Newman's *Idea of a University* may require some reshaping to meet the demands of 1990. As

President Howell and Professor Eidson of Central Methodist College have said in their book, "At the ideal liberal arts college there will be a *wedding of values to utility.*"[1]

5. The United Methodist Church should undertake to help its local congregations understand that a Christian college is not, and cannot be, an extended Sunday school or a reformatory where the mistakes and neglect of parents are overcome. Our people need to grasp the fact that the Christian college must value genuine academic freedom as a religious principle.

6. United Methodism should undertake all necessary efforts to assist our General Board of Higher Education and Ministry in providing a permanent endowment of at least $100,000,000 (the fund is already well under way), the earnings from which will be committed to scholarship assistance for the youth of our denomination. This will enable thousands of United Methodist young people to seek their education in our own Christian colleges.

7. If diminishing private philanthropy, because of tax revision, becomes critical for Christian colleges, some appropriate approach to public funds (with necessary safeguards to protect the colleges' independence) may need to be considered by The United Methodist Church. There are many instances already where federal and state sources are subsidizing tuition costs. However, the improbable irony of the current predicament is that the government has now acted to limit the possibility of private gifts at the same time it has withdrawn many of its scholarships and other grants. When I became a college president in 1956, it was unthinkable that the public sector of higher education should invade private philanthropy deliberately and overtly, or that the private sector should seek public funds. Now the old rubric has been changed—both ways. If there is a serious lessening of private gifts, the Christian college may have to invoke its new right to solicit in the public domain, in order to guarantee its future.

8. United Methodism, with some of its family of institutions in serious financial straits, may need to consider an honorable closing of certain colleges in the larger interest of sustaining healthier units, particularly where there are both kinds drawing upon the financial resources of a single annual conference.

The "Glory of the Lighted Mind"

My own conviction about the theme developed in this chapter is so unshakable that I wish I could write it in letters of fire across the skies of United Methodism. If we love our country, if we cherish human freedoms, if we prize civilization itself, if we are dedicated to the eternal objectives of the Christian church, we will never as a denomination allow ourselves to lose aggressive interest in the glory of the lighted mind. Institutional Christian higher education is at the very center of our church's mission, and always will be if we remain sensitive to the insights of John Wesley, our founder and mentor who himself exemplified that combination of knowledge and vital piety of which his brother Charles wrote.

There is a lovely story among the legends of Emory and Henry College. Uncle Bob Sheffey, fabled circuit-riding evangelist of southwest Virginia, whose untutored pulpit eloquence is still remembered nearly a century after his death, was riding to an afternoon engagement near Galax, and stopped to worship at the eleven o'clock service in the Methodist Church there. Richard Green Waterhouse, then President of Emory and Henry College and later a bishop of the church, was the guest preacher. Uncle Bob tethered his horse, entered the sanctuary, and settled himself on the back pew just as Dr. Waterhouse was beginning his sermon, "Christian Higher Education." The host pastor noticed the colorful itinerant preacher squirming in his pew throughout the service and sensed that Uncle Bob must be feeling that any preacher who was compelled to use Christian higher education as his theme had to be totally out of gospel! Nevertheless, when the service was being concluded, he called on Brother Sheffey to come forward and pronounce the benediction. These were Uncle Bob's opening words: "O Lord, bless the *big* man who preached the *little* sermon!"

Perhaps our task continues to be that of helping our people—and our preachers—know that sermons and programs related to education in a Christian college are neither little nor inconsequential. Dean Lynn Harold Hough of Drew University said near the end of his life, "True evangelicalism is intelligence on fire," and it is constantly our challenge, and now our urgent duty, to help the church grasp this fact.

CHAPTER SEVEN

Overcoming the Paralysis of Structure

Structure can paralyze, but it doesn't need to do so. On Friday evening, January 15, 1886, a young man named John R. Mott walked into a meeting at Cornell University where the internationally famous Cricketeer J. E. K. Studd was speaking. Mott heard Studd's voice ring out in the words of Jesus, "Seekest thou great things for thyself? Seek them not. Seek ye first the kingdom of God." Mott was transfixed and found no peace until he was able to say, in the words of St. Thomas, "My Lord and my God!"

On Easter Sunday sixty-nine years later, John R. Mott, Nobel laureate, bowed with age and honored by the whole world, walked into my church in Morristown, Tennessee, on the arm of a relative whom he was visiting. After the service, while the congregation lingered in deference to its distinguished visitor, I escorted him from the sanctuary as he spoke to me animatedly of the resurrection gospel I had endeavored to preach. There was brightness in his eyes and eagerness in his voice while he told of his joy in having lived through nearly four score years and ten "strengthened with might by God's spirit in the inner man."

This best known of Methodist laypeople in this century, for all of his authentic but humble saintliness, may have been the most inveterate organizer and builder of structures the Christian world has ever known. The YMCA, the Student Volunteer Movement, the International Missionary Council, and particularly the World Council of Churches, with their intricately pragmatic designs come to mind as examples. Remembering John R. Mott's life and career would convince me, even if there were no other arguments, that *essential structure* in the Body of Christ *never needs to diminish or destroy genuine spirituality.*

To borrow the analysis of a former denominational executive, The United Methodist Church undertakes to conduct its far-flung mission under the guidance of four major *program* boards, two of which (the General Board of Global Ministries and the General Board of Discipleship) are actually *mega-boards,* and two *focus* boards (the General Board of Higher Education and Ministry and the General Board of Church and Society); two *advocacy* commissions (Religion and Race and Status and Role of Women); three *service* commissions (Archives and History, Communications, and Christian Unity and Interreligious Concerns); two *support* boards (Pensions and Publication); two *administrative councils* (the General Council on Ministries and the General Council on Finance and Administration); and two *constitutional* councils (the Council of Bishops and the Judicial Council). Because of the dimensions of our work around the world, there is necessarily an enormous amount of power concentrated in all of these structures.

In what some have discerned to be a power struggle for leadership within the denomination, the major program boards and the General Council on Ministries were seen for a while as being pitted against the Council of Bishops. This may have been partially a correct assessment of the situation during a period of time when the office of bishop was under sharp attack and when at least some of its occupants appeared to be more cautious than bold in the exercise of our constitutional function, giving the impression that we were afraid to lead the church. This competition, if it did exist, has now given way to a more collegial relationship between the bishops and the general boards.

Bigness begets structure or bureaucracy. If the early Christians had known that they were founding an organization to last for centuries, in all probability they would have organized it to death. However, since they believed that they were making simple provisional arrangements for a brief period of time, they left it free to live. When Methodism was a frontier movement whose preachers, dressed in deerskins and homespuns, traveled on horseback or afoot with no roads except Indian trails, preaching simply and straight from the heart the strong doctrines of repentance and grace, the need for organizational structure was minimal. But the very success of these first efforts mandated for their survival an increasing number of administrative arrangements, so it all began and so it has developed as our church has grown, until the bureaucracy we know today is basically the essential accompaniment of our bigness. The popular posture of a typical United Methodist, clergy or lay, famous or unknown, is traditionally critical if not contemptuous of our church's institutional hierarchy. One well-known exemplar of this attitude was the late Dr. Ralph W. Sockman, who deeply believed that "our ecclesiastical structures are top heavy."[1] I seriously doubt if any bishop of our church would disagree in principle with this statement.

There is more, however, to be said on the subject. John Wesley himself, with all of his intentional spirituality, had an incurable predilection for organization. Indeed, when he and his brother Charles formed the Holy Club at Oxford University, its patterns of structure and discipline were so visible as to cause those outside that inner circle to apply to its members, almost derisively, the name "Methodists," which later attached itself permanently to Wesley's followers. In addition to other explanations for the endurance of the fellowship emanating from the life and thought of the great Oxonian, surely one factor not to be overlooked is the simple but practical structures he proposed and helped to implement. Wesley preached to win converts, but when they had been won, he gathered them into classes and arranged for them to come under an appropriate discipline to assure their spiritual growth and to enable them to enjoy the encouragement of warmhearted Christian fellowship in the process.

His distinguished contemporary, George Whitefield, a more eloquent preacher than Wesley ever was, never did this. Magnificent in his ability to move crowds from the pulpit or in the open air, Whitefield depended solely upon the power of his sermon and gave little or no thought to what should come afterward. He said near the end of his life, "My brother Wesley acted wisely. The souls that were awakened under his ministry he joined in class, and thus preserved the fruit of his labours. This I neglected, and my people are a rope of sand."[2]

Charles W. Ferguson, the editor and diplomat who analyzed the structural genius of Methodism in his book *Organizing to Beat the Devil,* has called our attention to "the interstitial connection between [Methodism] and the nation that has been its host." He writes:

> Quite possibly, for example, not a few of the regulatory practices of a body of people devoutly methodical affect American social habits and procedures. The combination of exuberance and statistics that belongs to the national scene, of idealism and bureaucracy, of ponderous effort and quick wit, of grandiose plans and infinite detail—all may arise out of forces of which Methodist churches in their various branches are a part, if not indeed the chief exemplar. . . . The current Methodist term *administrivia* illustrates an awareness of this combination within the denomination, as does the saying that the Greeks had a word for it and the Methodists have a pamphlet for it.[3]

Bishop Tuell, in his excellent book *The Organization of the United Methodist Church,* reminds us that the design of our church "grows out of several factors: (1) we are ministering to a complex world, (2) we want to have as many people as possible participate in decision-making, and (3) we want to create methods of accountability."[4]

How does a veteran of more than thirty years of relationship to our bureaucratic structure undertake to assess it? At least two hundred times I have seen a conglomerate company of preachers, bishops, homemakers, lawyers, judges, doctors, educators, business women and men, farmers, editors, public office holders, and youth, always interracial and now international, a beautiful mixture of sophisticates and plain people, sit down together to grapple with issues and programs that affect us all. We have discovered an easy camaraderie stretching across the lines of vocation, race, sex, and status, and have attacked almost voraciously literally mountains of printed and mimeographed materials in a brave attempt to separate quality from quantity and to identify real issues in the midst of proliferated rhetoric. I must admit that, like the good United

Methodists we are, we have nearly always approached our tasks with rollicking eagerness, seeming to take to the labyrinth of bureaucratic duties as the proverbial duck takes to water!

There have been boring, wearying sessions, to be sure; but there have been high moments, too: a general secretary's report shot through with bold vision and prophecy; a comment wrenched from the heart of a board member painfully concerned for his or her church "back home"; a prayer that brought heaven very close to West End Church's room 207; a devotional that moved us past tomes of talk and brought the Bible's clarion call on some issue straight to our souls with shattering power.

From all my years of involvement in the structures of our church, I may have earned the right to venture certain observations:

1. Bureaucracy is necessary in a church as large as ours, and part of our task as United Methodist disciples is to learn to appreciate it and to help make it what it should and can be.

2. Bureaucracy, i.e., the great boards and other agencies of the church, must strive deliberately and intentionally to know and understand the concerns of grass-roots United Methodism and to take its agonies and ecstasies into honest consideration when significant issues are being decided and important pronouncements crafted.

3. The agencies must remember always that they never speak *for* the church, but only *to* it. On the other hand, our people must realize that their general agencies are divinely impelled to speak prophetically to them, and they must become willing to hear and ponder their messages.

4. The great boards must never move too far ahead of where the people are, and they must be willing to listen sincerely to input from intelligent conservatives as well as liberals among their members and throughout the church.

5. All of our agencies, of course, must administer faithfully the actions of General Conference, even when those actions are not pleasing to them. It perplexes the church and destroys the credibility of boards and agencies when directors or staffs, albeit subtly, work in behalf of positions contrary to those taken by General Conference. It is true, as all responsible leaders

know, that the position one occupies on occasion may properly impose restraints on what one might otherwise be free to say and do. Too, the integrity of the image of all boards and agencies requires the exercise of meticulous care and faithfulness in the administration of authorized funds, always with an overarching consciousness of what the General Conference has declared to be its will.

6. All boards and agencies must deal faithfully, promptly, and courteously with the least as well as the greatest of our constituents, answering mail punctually, responding willingly and if possible helpfully to important and unimportant queries, and striving to build and keep intact mutually beneficial relationships.

7. The significance of the *church press* must be interpreted constantly to our people and their reading of it encouraged and made economically feasible, in order that their understanding of the church and its actions may be as accurate as possible. The readiness of the *secular press,* with its predictable ignorance of the manner in which the church operates, to dramatize the more sensational or "newsworthy" of general board pronouncements is the source of much harmful ferment. Such stories in the secular press, perhaps innocently, often succeed in making actions taken by our agencies *appear* to be the equivalent of official positions of the denomination that can be determined only by General Conference.

8. Our general boards and agencies must be fully aware of the enormous responsibility that rests on them because their staffs, with background knowledge and ample time for such highly technical tasks, compose a large portion of the legislation presented to General Conference. They must exercise extraordinary integrity to guarantee that the discharge of this duty involves not simply agency perspectives but a sincere effort to provide fairly for broader denominational concerns.

9. I would suggest that our boards and agencies consider whether or not a reduction in the number of staff members present at General Conference, sometimes for purposes of lobbying, might create a favorable reaction within the church and accomplish needed economy, as well as help purify the political process by enabling General Conference delegates to

form their judgments more objectively. I know the need for resource people who can provide essential information.

10. The boards and agencies of the church must nurture constantly a capacity for *self-criticism* and so resist the temptations that accompany power.

11. The all-important and all-powerful nominating process by which the composition of boards and agencies is meant to be determined on an equitable and representative basis must make certain that the directors named always include a fair number of able and intelligent men and women of more *conservative religious and political perspectives*. They, too, are loyal and competent United Methodists. Because I myself come from the more liberal tradition of our church (a tradition that likewise must always be represented) I have noticed again and again that the nominating process has seemed to fall short at this point—a failure that would not and should not be tolerated in the case of representation of ethnics, women, or those of different age groups.

Let me attempt now to address certain "myths" that I have heard with regard to United Methodist bureaucracy:

1. Some say that the staffs of general boards and agencies are not active in attendance at worship and in the programs of local churches where they reside. My own years as bishop of the Nashville Area revealed to me that our churches in Nashville, large and small, numbered among *their most responsible leaders* (members of administrative boards, councils on ministries, choirs, committees, and Sunday school teachers) those from the professional and support staffs of the general agencies based in that city. On the whole, I have not encountered a more deeply dedicated or more helpful group of churchmen and churchwomen than those who belong to the general staffs of our church with which I have been associated.

2. Some suggest that the board and agency staffs are *refugees from the itinerancy* who could never succeed as ministers or lay employees in local churches. Most of those whom I know have been selected carefully in a highly competitive process and represent remarkable talent that already has made its distinguished mark on the local church or annual conference level, or on both.

3. Some insist that board and agency staffs are unconcerned or uninformed about the local church. Again, those whom I have known are the opposite; they have become intentionally familiar with the local church, and its welfare and growth are the main goals of their professional lives.

Some of the finest Christians I have ever known in my denomination have been identified creatively with the bureaucracy of the church. I name a representative few from those now retired or deceased: Myron F. Wicke, Eugene L. Smith, George Outen, Thelma Stevens, Harry Haines, Betsy Ewing, John O. Gross, Harry Denman, and Gerald O. McCullough. It may be an unfortunate reality that our persistent prejudice against the ecclesiastical structure of our church has kept us from giving proper recognition or expressing appropriate gratitude to a distinguished and able company of Christian leaders who serve us well in often thankless ways.

A Special Concern

This chapter would fail in its intentional candor if it neglected to deal particularly with one of the current situations existing in United Methodism. I refer to the present controversy over two different philosophies of mission, one held by the General Board of Global Ministries and the other by the Mission Society for United Methodists which came into existence prior to the 1984 General Conference. I approach this discussion with a full awareness that the problem is difficult, delicate, and complex, but with the hope that concerned church leaders like myself may find a way to bring a desperately needed reconciliation between these viewpoints.

The Board of Global Ministries has emerged as the most controversial of the general boards of our church, partly because of its immense size and the wide scope of its programs. Another and perhaps more substantive reason has been its own gradual adoption of a *philosophy of mission* that represents something quite different from that held by the church in the past. Historically, we have believed in the primacy of winning individuals to Jesus Christ, with efforts related to the changing of social and political orders following in due course. More recently the Board of Global Ministries *seems* to have adopted as a primary objective infiltrating and changing political and social orders, with a secondary emphasis on winning people to Christ.

This shift in declared goals and priorities has resulted in the reallocation of vast amounts of money, in a startling reduction of the number of missionary personnel maintained in the field (another reason for this latter change is the fortunate indigenization of local church leadership in mission lands) and in widespread misunderstanding on the part of many United Methodist people. The Board of Global Ministry's sincere dedication to the poor and oppressed, I believe, has led sometimes to an uncritical acceptance of liberation theology and likewise to what seems to many to be an unfair evaluation of our own national situation as opposed to that of socialist countries.

The serious questioning of current policies and programs of the Board of Global Ministries came to a head in 1983 when a group of prominent pastors and mission scholars, together with certain laity, formed the Mission Society for United Methodists as an alternative sending agency. The Society sought but did not receive General Conference endorsement in 1984. However, the General Conference requested the Council of Bishops to engage the opposing groups in dialogue and to attempt reconciliation of the two viewpoints.

The bishops, in their Episcopal Address to the 1984 General Conference, unequivocally declared their support of the Board of Global Ministries as the "sole sending agency of missionaries," disapproving the organization of another sending agency in competition with it.[5] *But they added this statement:* "However, in fairness to the concerns of those who feel the necessity for a second agency, we urge that measures be taken to assure our people that evangelization and evangelism are a vital part of the philosophy and practice of mission by the Board and *that its staff is committed to Wesleyan theology.*"[6]

I must say at this point that the observations included in this section about a special concern are essentially those of one who has been totally outside the process of dialogue designed to effect reconciliation. Many conversations were held, and it was determined that a covenant of strictest confidentiality would be observed by all parties. I was at no time a part of these discussions, and my perspective on the controversy, as a result, may possess the objectivity of noninvolvement while lacking the accuracy of involvement. Any analysis that I would venture represents strictly my own thinking. With that necessary stipulation, I offer the following observations.

1. I wish to speak a very positive word about the effectiveness of BGM's almost unbelievably varied ministries. Granted the negative feelings with which most of us have grappled in recent years, any fair-minded survey of the worldwide program presided over by this great general board would afford abundant cause for rejoicing. A visit to many developing countries would reveal splendid rapport between the board and their bishops and a rich variety of constructive, creative projects under way. The humanitarian ministry being accomplished by UMCOR and the exciting miracles wrought by the Advance are literally incalculable in their significance. We are all beneficiaries of the National Division's rich resources for local churches and annual conferences, particularly in the areas of church development, fund raising, and skillful, imaginative strategies designed to increase United Methodism's effectiveness in building ministries to this nation's growing variety of ethnic communities.

2. It appears at this point that neither BGM nor the Mission Society has been able to reach an acceptable level of trust toward the other, although there have been some signs of modest progress. As an outsider I have seen no evidence of willingness on the part of either group to compromise enough to make eventual reconciliation a viable possibility.

3. While the current controversy remains unresolved within the general church, one could hope that each party would conduct itself in such a manner as to create mutual respect, and, therefore, minimize the possibility that the issue will be settled finally on any basis other than that of biblical and theological merit. Put another way, every effort should be made by the leaders of both groups to eliminate the indictment of individuals and the use of the world's mission theaters for political advantage, in order that the church's consideration

of the total problem may be kept as objective as possible.

4. One option open to BGM would be to recognize the existence of the Mission Society and its operation, provided the Society would be willing for such an arrangement and provided both agencies would honor such a covenant and cease criticizing each other. At best this would acknowledge the diversity of viewpoints on mission existing in United Methodism. At worst it would solve no basic problems and, in spite of good intentions, could perpetuate a subterranean competitiveness likely at any time to erupt in a new crisis. The question of its legality would need to be faced, in view of the General Conference's declaration in favor of a *single* sending agency.

5. The Mission Society for United Methodists, in my judgment, could find its future existence increasingly difficult to finance and uncertain to plan. The goodwill it can claim in grass-roots United Methodism is unorganized, and the task of pitting itself constantly against such a strong entity as BGM may prove ever more formidable and discouraging. If its *basic cause* is the issue most important in its thinking, the Society might be well advised to cultivate a willingness on the part of BGM to meet its fundamental requirements and, if and when this is done, to consider its own honorable dissolution. Unless the humanness that is part of our fallen nature should dictate the retention of an organization to satisfy purposes of pride (and I would pray this might not be the case), such a sequence of healing events ought to be a possibility.

6. There may have been a tendency by BGM to classify the differences of judgment and perspective represented by the Mission Society as being basically of "Good News" origin, and therefore not to be identified with a numerically significant segment of United Methodism. Such thinking, in my opinion, requires review. The evangelical renaissance is a religious fact of our times, now established historically in a manner quite beyond question. It is not a sectarian or national phenomenon; rather it is ecumenical (including Roman Catholic) and international. Our own Good News Movement, sometimes referred to as our church's evangelical caucus, is but a *very small manifestation* of a far wider reality in the Christian world. It is voicing concerns, sometimes in different phraseology, of

multiplied numbers of United Methodist people who are not, and will never be, identified with it as an organization.

Here I must insert an important parenthesis. With some personalities and episodes excepted, I am convinced that the Good News Movement (of which I myself have never been a part) has been essentially beneficial to our denomination. It has given a voice to an authentic contingent of United Methodism too frequently silenced by more vocal liberal leadership and has served as a corrective influence when streams of doctrine, polity, and program have sought to overrun the banks of historical balance.

The Good News Movement has maintained consistent loyalty to The United Methodist Church, surely against sometimes militant urgings to the contrary, a fact inadequately recognized by our church leaders. It undoubtedly commands respect far beyond the circle of its own adherents.

All of us, because we are bound hopelessly by our creaturehood, must articulate the deep concerns of our souls within the limitations imposed by our human predilection to pettiness and prejudice—something I know experientially.

So it is that I venture here a pastoral word to my friends of the Good News Movement, with the full awareness that I must hear it first myself. It is a necessary warning to *all* followers of Jesus Christ regardless of their creedal persuasions.

Those committed and zealous Christians who belong to United Methodism's evangelical caucus, in spite of their commendable insistence on neglected Wesleyan doctrines and priorities, need to guard vigilantly against narrow, bigoted theological thinking, against the neurosis of malignant negativism, and against a dangerous form of Pharisaism quick to assume a judgmental posture—sometimes without accurate or adequate information and often without the amelioration of Christian love. They, like all of us, must strive for positive, compassionate fairness in acts of complaint as well as praise.

It is true that for many years *we have accepted and even welcomed other special interest caucuses* into the life of our church. Most of us would acknowledge that, while they have occasionally brought unrest to our comfortably settled notions, in the end they have focused our attention and thought on areas of concern we almost certainly had been guilty of neglecting and would have continued to neglect without their Spirit-led prodding. Why can we not think of the Good News Movement in a similar way, and so thank God for it?

7. The Board of Global Ministries, like any agency of the church, must hear the legitimate concerns of its critics, and show readiness to effect *substantive* changes in policy and program, and possibly in personnel, in order to satisfy persistent questions coming from wider sources than any evangelical caucus. Each of our agencies must demonstrate willing accountability to the *whole* church, and not simply engage in vocal maneuvers that do not contemplate any actual revision in present positions. As has already been stated, the 1984 Episcopal Address, together with the action of the General Conference, mandated a *serious* effort to produce reconciliation on the vital issue of the church's mission enterprise. This is vastly important for the health of United Methodism.

8. It would be neither necessary nor right to alter or abandon present excellent programs sponsored by the Board of Global Ministry in order to approach a reconciliation of viewpoints within our church. What *may* be needed is for BGM to augment its current efforts with a bold new design for the evangelization of individuals and personnel to achieve it. Added to this should be an honest openness to the historic evangelical perspective; a demonstrated willingness to receive qualified evangelical missionary candidates; and the appointment of able, cooperative, even distinguished representatives of this viewpoint to significant executive positions in the board where they would share properly in its policy-making and administrative processes. If we, indeed, are to recognize the diversity within our church, some such action, in my judgment, is required to restore confidence and unity.

9. General boards can become so large and powerful that they are virtually unmanageable. Particularly is this true in terms of the General Council on Ministries' disciplinary responsibility to monitor the program boards. Too, they can, over the years, acquire financial resources of such magnitude that their dependence on the World Service dollar is lessened

dramatically, and as an inevitable consequence their sense of obligation to the supporting church significantly diminished. I am not competent to make a recommendation here, but I venture the thought that there may be a point at which United Methodism should consider again a *more decentralized,* and therefore more readily responsible bureaucratic structure, especially in the case of the large program boards.

10. It should be remembered by all of us who are United Methodists, including leaders of BGM and the Mission Society, that ultimate decisions with regard to the mission philosophy of our denomination are made not by any of us, but by General Conference. If the current controversy cannot be resolved otherwise, then its resolution needs to be accomplished by future General Conferences. In our nation, given its present mood of political and social conservatism, the problem itself is not likely to go away.

11. A church that has been bold enough to issue a strong statement calling for reconciliation among the peoples of the world ought to accord first priority to the matter of achieving such within its own household. It would be the finest hour in its long and noble history for the General Board of Global Ministries, through its own governors and staff, to assume decisive and visible initiative in restructuring its program to satisfy the *legitimate* concerns of all United Methodists who still believe, as Bishop Newbigin says forcefully in a new book, that human culture must be evangelized by confronting it with a Damascus Road experience.[7] It is of utmost importance to secure basic agreement on the nature of the mission of The United Methodist Church, if the confidence of our people is to be restored in its vital programs. *This is surely not too much to expect or require of mature Christians!*

About Electing Bishops

Thus far in this chapter I have spoken strictly about bureaucracy. I now must express a conviction that I hold about the office of bishop. I am hesitant to do this because I do not have an alternative proposal; however, there may be some value simply in stating the problem.

I am opposed to the present method being used in our Jurisdictional Conferences (I cannot speak for the Central Conferences) to elect men and women to the episcopacy. It politicizes the process in a way that can easily prevent a superior but unsponsored person from being chosen. It enables the larger annual conferences to pool their votes by previous agreement and so control ballots, thus virtually eliminating the equally important chances of smaller conferences to promote able and worthy prospects. If the procedure of asking "candidates" to appear before delegations for statements and subsequent interrogation is employed, it tends to diminish the dignity and perhaps even to compromise the integrity of these men and women. Most important of all, the Holy Spirit must enter this process, if at all, in a roundabout and uncertain way!

I acknowledge gratefully that many excellent individuals have been elected while this process has been in vogue, but I still feel that its principle is more political than Christian, and that there are within it the latent dangers of mediocrity and, much worse, tragic error.

I also recognize that voting delegates must have ways of learning about those clergy who are in consideration for the episcopacy, but I believe such can be devised without the use of overt public interviews.

I belong to a generation that at its best believed the office should seek the person, and not the person the office; and to a vanishing company of bishops who were elected in a manner that may not have been entirely pure but one that had not reached the level of political maneuvering we know today. Judge Tom Matheny of our present Judicial Council wrote a perceptive article on this subject in *Circuit Rider*.[8] Matheny advocated a specific plan to reform episcopal elections, including the abolition of caucuses, annual conference candidates, and campaign literature and, positively, the creation of a workable mechanism to identify qualified leaders, and a *changing of the atmosphere* "of the whole process" from the election of delegates to the conduct of Jurisdictional Conferences. It is a radical but provocative proposal.

Conclusion

How does a great denomination avoid the perils of complex structure, the dangers of bureaucracy? One answer is obvious: by having as little of that structure as is possible. This, I think, must always be in the mind of United Methodism's leadership, and particularly its General Conferences.

Another response should be equally apparent: by remembering that, in the end, it is the *local church* that matters supremely. All administrative structure, all bureaucracy, all hierarchy, are its servants or else they are unable to defend their presence.

When I go into a little sanctuary in the inner city of one of Florida's great metropolitan centers on Sunday morning and gaze into faces, many of which are lined with suffering and weary with disillusionment, I invariably recall that my very office exists for them. I am one of their pastors, one of their teachers, one called to make the Lord Jesus Christ more a reality in their lives. The throbbing dynamics at work in that coterie of believers (not the pageantry of General Conference, not the deliberative procedures of a great board in annual session, not the studied dignity of a Council of Bishops meeting) is *where the vital life of the church really is and where the future of God's kingdom lies.*

Finally, and perhaps most difficult, United Methodism must try desperately and constantly to *spiritualize* its whole complex bureaucratic structure. It must combine organizational skills with soul-searching, heartwarming religion in much the same way John R. Mott did across a busy lifetime that left new boroughs of the City of God over all the earth.

That unique Dutch Catholic Christian, Father Henri J. M. Nouwen, who has made such an impact on the thinking of contemporary Christianity, wrote in his book *The Wounded Healer* a chapter entitled "Ministry for a Rootless Generation."[9] In this chapter, although dealing with the theme of ministry, Nouwen gave a helpful summary of what I mean when I offer the audacious proposal to spiritualize the witness of United Methodist structures. He spoke of three roles for the Christian minister of the future: the *first* had to do with the minister as "the articulator of inner events." Nouwen deplored the fact that Christian leaders think in terms of "large-scale organizations . . . and running the show as circus directors."[10] He pleaded for ministers, surely lay as well as clerical, able to give guidance where the interior life is concerned and to share with others their own experiences of spiritual reality. The *second* role saw the minister as a person of *compassion.* Nouwen wrote of that craving for love that a human being has in his or her own heart, and the privilege of the Christian leader to guide a person into forgiveness, to bring out the best in that individual, and to motivate that person to go forward toward a more human community. *Finally,* Nouwen spoke of the minister as a *contemplative* person. Here he envisioned the Christian's ability to look beyond immediate events and situations and to keep glimpsing "the new world beyond the veil of everyday life." This, surely, is the hope and promise of any human situation, the infinite possibility of faith itself.

Is it too much to challenge ourselves with the idea of making our intricate organizational structures *instruments* leading us in the direction of more authentic *spiritual* ministry? This would transform the workshop and the laboratory into a sanctuary and would inform the sanctuary with the essential results achieved in the workshop and the laboratory. So may even bureaucracy experience sanctification. So may it rise triumphantly, but always humbly, above its own structures. And so, bless God, may it lose itself in that larger service for the last and the least of those for whom a Savior died!

CHAPTER EIGHT
Where the Real Issues Lie

Bishop Roy H. Short, assessing the intricate complexity of the human and societal problems with which the Christian Church in its effort to be faithful struggles today, has observed whimsically that he can remember when one of the largest questions with which the people of God were dealing was whether or not women should be permitted to bob their hair! This is an impressive commentary on the radical change that has come in the church's interpretation of its mission in the lifetime of one distinguished leader because of the cluster of revolutions that have converged on the human scene in recent decades. It is a tribute to the power of the gospel that the consciences of men and women committed to Jesus Christ have been sharpened at so many points and that they have sought in multiple ways to stand boldly and courageously in behalf of righteousness and justice for the entire human family. While it may seem true to some people that the church has prospered statistically more when it has elected noninvolvement in the great socio-political issues of today's world, United Methodism at its best has repudiated this argument and sought to make its presentation of the gospel both personal and social.

The impetus of our intense and wide efforts has sometimes caused United Methodism (and other mainline denominations as well) to concentrate its energies and resources on the accomplishment of social objectives with a resulting neglect of personal ministries. Our critics have claimed that we have worn for more than thirty years the trappings of a spiritually arid activism accomplished too often at the expense of theological breadth and depth, philosophical and psychological maturity, and authentic devotional reflection and that our activism has become nearly monstrous, often incompletely informed, sometimes politically biased, and frequently without clear logic and dependable consistency. The emphasis has been on *doing* instead of *being*. We have produced a cacophony of loud, sometimes well-worded outcries, fashioned into resolutions often more political than religious in context, about nearly every human issue worthy of headlines. Some would say that more frequently than not the results have been distressingly poor; the church has lost depth and the body politic has not been impressed! Put another way, the controversial involvement of the church in a thousand and one social/political struggles around the globe has seemed to produce little change in the bottom line report on the human malady. Its cost effectiveness has been virtually nil.

But while there is some accuracy in such an analysis, faithful United Methodist leaders know that it does not tell the whole story. Jesus spoke with clear vehemence to the Pharisees and the Sadducees, as recorded in the opening verses of the sixteenth chapter of Matthew's Gospel, deploring the fact that they were able to search the skies for evidence of the kind of weather to be expected, but incapable of studying the circumstances and events of their own history in a manner that would help them comprehend the signs of the times.

When an honest history of the modern church is written, undoubtedly it will record the fact that the enduring health of the Christian movement in the twentieth century was achieved more by the sincere, if costly, involvement of the people of God in efforts to better the human situation, than by the kind of intentional ecclesiastical isolation that produces statistical triumphs and popular accolades. It is the old and valid religious principle of placing spiritual faithfulness above worldly success. Our commitment to this principle has made me proud to be a United Methodist.

But we must keep a sense of balance. While struggling in all legitimate ways to influence society in the holy directions of peace, justice, and righteousness, we must never forget that the core of Christian teaching has always insisted on *being* as the essential parent of effective *doing*, and our commitment to a *whole evangelism* and a *conscious cultivation of the inner spiritual life* must never be permitted to slacken. This has to mean that our choice of issues to command the attention of United Methodism must be made with great care and must include those related to individual Christian growth as well as world problems. The leadership of our church must try to discern the signs of our times objectively and accurately, and with an honest effort not to allow their discernment to be distorted by personal prejudice, commitment to preferential issues, or inflexible preconceptions. All of us must be sure that we know where the *real issues* lie. Our people have the right to expect this from us.

Let me comment, as a single United Methodist individual, on a modest catalog of problems with which I myself am convinced today's United Methodism should concern itself.

1. *The widespread impression that United Methodism has abandoned doctrinal conviction and emphasis.* Many leaders will disavow this, but strong evidence supports the fact that great numbers of our members have deep concern at this point. We must make a deliberate effort to bring our message about personal salvation and spiritual help for the everyday problems of life into visible balance with our social pronouncements and programs. I do not attempt to elaborate my statement of this need, but I place it first among the problems I am convinced must be addressed. Our churches will never experience dramatic growth, especially among young and middle adults, until they preach and teach a gospel that ministers to ordinary human needs, including guilt and fear, in today's complex society.

2. *The persistent problem of ministerial incompetence.* The patience of many laypeople who long for their churches to be what they should be is wearing dangerously thin because annual conferences, sometimes repeatedly, have assigned professionally incompetent ministers to their pulpits. Some ministers, while of excellent character, clearly lack the essential gifts and graces of their calling. Our *sent* ministry with its guaranteed appointments is the basis for this problem. It is possible for professional incompetence to be rewarded with years of successive (sometimes steadily improving) appointments, to the detriment of a series of local churches. This may occur

(rarely) because of the political exigencies of the appointment-making process, but it appears more often because it is difficult, embarrassing, and occasionally cruel to provide a way of exit for a minister who is morally clean but simply cannot do the job.

Business and industry have means of dealing with incompetence, but United Methodism seems to lack such capability. Part of this is traceable to the fact that the church is motivated by Christian love in dealing with its ministers; however, the welfare of the church itself must always supersede all else.

Three approaches suggest themselves. First, boards of ordained ministry *must* tighten the entrance process into annual conference membership. Second, bishops and cabinets must have the courage to deal decisively with ministerial incompetence. Third, the process of implementing administrative location must be refined and improved constantly, with the initiative always belonging to the bishop and cabinet. Appeal for appropriate review should be possible in the event of unfairness.

Failure to provide an honorable, although involuntary exit route for those ministers not equipped to perform their tasks will mean, in my judgment, the certain conclusion of guaranteed appointments in United Methodism.

3. *The lingering vestiges of racism and sexism in the church.* Perhaps the phrase "lingering vestiges" is overly optimistic. There is still *much* to be done, but some progress has been made, and the consciousness of The United Methodist Church has been raised on both of these issues in a manner that promises better days ahead.

We have integrated racially, to some extent at least, the higher and many of the lower structural levels of The United Methodist Church, but often at the expense of leadership desperately needed for local congregations. Although it has made for a meaningful witness to the ecumenical church and the world, it may in the end harbor the seeds of mortal error. Our ethnic churches, particularly the Black congregations—as is said elsewhere in these pages—do not possess vigorous spiritual health and as a group, when the Koreans are excluded, are showing poor growth in terms of population expansion. We have not yet determined for ourselves how to reconcile our commitment to racially integrated congregations with our apparently necessary support of ethnically segregated churches. The problems of cultural differences, varying forms of worship and persistent traditions are so formidable that this reconciliation may not be within reach in the foreseeable future. Many of our churches are moving in the direction of racially integrated memberships: at the time of this writing approximately 370 of the 733 churches in the Florida Conference alone are integrated. Some of this integration is "token," but some is far more substantive. The attitudes of our people seem to be undergoing a gradual but sure change at this point.

Honest white United Methodists know that an unconscious but dangerous racist perspective is still deeply ingrained in their minds and habit patterns. It will be less true as younger generations come on the scene, but most of us who are older and still exert influence in the life of the church need desperately the regenerating and sanctifying power of the Holy Spirit to exorcise from our inner beings subsconscious attitudes and reactions that keep us from being totally the children of God. The work of the church and the intentional efforts of its leaders must continue until total racial justice is a realized fact in United Methodism's life.

Part of our international witness against racism must be continued vigorous protest to the South African government for its reprehensible policy of *apartheid*. Running like a strong thread through the program of the 1986 World Methodist Conference in Nairobi, Kenya, was the daily witness of nearly 3,000 people and their featured speakers, among whom was Archbishop Tutu, against this incredible wrong. United Methodism and the entire Christian community must influence more and more of the governments of the earth to help rid the people of South Africa of this human plague.

An honest reading of Scripture and Christian history would confirm that the elevation of womanhood and the slow evolution of its rights and prerogatives have definite Christian origins. Far greater progress toward these goals and a vastly energized consciousness on the part of citizens and church members have come in recent years, for which all of us should thank God! Progress has not been as rapid in some parts of the world as it has been here. We should be particularly grateful for our church's enthusiastic authorization of the ordination of women and their acceptance as ministerial members of annual conferences. There are now also female bishops and district superintendents, and there will be many more in days ahead.

Too, we should be grateful for the fact that an increasing number of ministers and members in our denomination are making faithful efforts to speak inclusively in sermons and conversations. Unfortunately, for some this is still a shore dimly seen and much progress is yet needed. I believe that the sleeping conscience of our great church on matters such as these is awakening slowly but surely, and that the leadership of our denomination is basically committed to all of the valid insistences of the feminist movement, including appropriate revision in the wording of many beloved hymns of the church and of its liturgies and prayers.

To be honest—and this is one of the controlling purposes of this book—I must record my own belief that the language revision promoted by some leaders in the current movement should not extend to Scripture under any circumstances. My first reason for saying this is my own commitment to accuracy of translations and integrity of scholarship. We have spent centuries attempting to bring to the Christian community authentic versions of the original scriptural autographs. To rewrite portions of this painstaking work in a way that actually makes the Bible say what the early papyri never did say, it seems to me, is to prostitute biblical scholarship and to go far beyond our proper prerogatives. Most of the references to God in the Bible are masculine, but surely our human intelligence permits us to understand that they are to be taken as generic. They do not have to be changed for me to know that God has the characteristics of motherhood as well as fatherhood. If they should be altered, even with noble intention, the problem of communicating the message of the gospel to the splendid plain people who are really grass-roots United Methodists would become much more difficult if not, indeed, insurmountable, and the focus would be on a marginal rather than a central issue.

Another concern has troubled me. Every important movement of human history has had its extremists, who often have done their cause more harm than good and so delayed its ultimate victory. Implicit in the more radical insistences that *some* leaders of the feminist movement have articulated are grave dangers to the integrity and even survival of the Christian family. I have observed complications from this problem to be factors in the break-up of some clergy and clergy couple marriages. The tension between vocational and career freedom and faithful pursuit of the roles of spouse and parent constitutes a delicate and complex issue that only total love, the highest human wisdom, and patient determination can resolve successfully. However, let me set the record straight; my own exposure to the more authentic and wiser leaders of the movement for women's rights within The United Methodist Church has brought me, on nearly every occasion, reassurance that they have been able to combine their own commitments to the feminine cause with faithful family membership.

Obviously, there is still a long unfinished agenda for United Methodists in the arenas of racial justice and equality for women, and we must get on with the task. It ought to shame us that all of this was not long since completed, for the principles involved are not only basic Christian ones, but also, for those of us who are citizens of the United States, concepts present either implicitly or explicitly in the foundation documents of our country. It is a scandal, when other urgent human problems clamor for our energy and resources, that we must still spend precious time and money doing work that by now should belong to the past!

4. *The peril of a nuclear holocaust.* Albert Einstein observed perceptibly that "the unleashed power of the atom has changed everything except the way we think." In 1945 there were *two* nuclear bombs; now there are more than *50,000* either deployed or stockpiled, many of which would make the bomb dropped over Hiroshima (which incinerated 140,000 human beings in a single blinding flash) seem less than the pop of a toy pistol. Every major city in the USSR is targeted, as is every major city in the United States. It is estimated that the first regular exchange of nuclear warfare would leave dead one

hundred million persons in our country, one hundred million in the Soviet Union, and an additional one hundred million in the European theater. There are *at least* thirty-five nations today capable of producing nuclear weapons, and we are told that there will be seventy by the year 2000. If present trends continue, the military budget of the United States soon will be equal to what the military budget of the entire world was a handful of years ago.

Jonathan Schell was right when he envisioned earth's sophisticated civilization as being replaced suddenly by "a republic of insects and grass."[1] It should be easy for our own pragmatic intelligence to sense that the people of God in all nations must strive to thwart the dangers of nuclear annihilation, or else the far-flung missional and evangelistic plans of the kingdom of God will be destroyed instantly, and long before their realization.

Many of those who write to me, including good United Methodist people, declare that the politics of international redemption from the nuclear danger is *not* the gospel's concern. I challenge this viewpoint theologically. God created his perfect world. Then came sin and, to use Milton's powerful figure, Lucifer, son of the morning, fell as lightning from heaven to become the prince of darkness. In the fullness of time God sent his Son Jesus Christ to restore his lost creation and to reinstate the divine dream. When one visits Westminster Abbey, he or she will see emblazoned over the high altar the promise of Revelation 11:15: "The kingdoms of this world are become the kingdoms of our Lord, and of his Christ" (KJV). When demonic forces in any land threaten the realization of the Creator's own plans for the destiny of this earth, the prevention of such a cosmic disaster becomes, theologically, the urgent business of the entire church.

While he was still a member of the Council of Bishops, my friend James Armstrong handed me, during one of our sessions, a scrap of verse whose author I do not know:

> Little man, little man,
> Where have you been?
> Farther and farther
> Than ever was seen.

> Little man, little man,
> What did you there?
> I awakened the atom
> Asleep in its lair.
>
> I shattered the atom
> And shuddered to find
> A power to destroy
> Or deliver mankind.
>
> In the lair of the atom
> Where no man had trod,
> I came upon Lucifer
> Challenging God.

The Council of Bishops of The United Methodist Church has joined the Roman Catholic bishops and such widely diverse individuals as the general secretaries and staffs of our own boards and agencies, Father Theodore Hesburgh of Notre Dame, Myron Augsburger, President David Hubbard of Fuller Theological Seminary and many of his colleagues, faculty members of Asbury Theological Seminary, Ted Engstrom of World Vision International, editor Jim Wallis of *Sojourners* magazine, *The Christian Century*'s editor James M. Wall, and evangelist Billy Graham in calling for a bold confrontation of the nuclear threat and the eventual destruction of nuclear arsenals. Their action received unexpected and tragic reinforcement by the peacetime disaster at Chernobyl with its far-reaching effects. Dr. Robert Gale, the American bone-marrow specialist who went to Russia to help in this crisis, has pointed out the mortal implications of a nuclear accident, reminding us that the difficulty and slowness of treating persons injured in the Chernobyl incident illustrated in a minor way the utter helplessness that would confront all of us in the event of *any* nuclear war. The bishops were not talking about an inadequate defense for our country, any more than they were denying or ignoring the Communist threat. These are entirely different matters. Governments, religion, education, the entire life existing upon this planet will be lost in cosmic memory if contemporary voices speaking against the continued proliferation of nuclear weapons are not heard.

Because I believe the Bible and am committed to help communicate its message throughout God's creation, I am convinced that it is both the right and the obligation of every United Methodist church, its minister and lay members, to speak with courage and integrity concerning the nuclear danger in our world today.

5. *The crisis of marriage and the home.* Nearly thirty years ago the late Dr. Carl Michalson, Andrew B. Stout Professor of Systematic Theology at Drew University until his untimely passing in 1965, wrote this paragraph:

> The most dramatic crisis of our day is taking place in the institution of marriage. Gradually the frequency of divorce is transforming the structure of marriage into a polygamous form. To be sure, it is only a "one-at-a-time polygamy" and it rarely adds up to more than deuterogamy. It is a social crisis, nonetheless, in which the character of a major institution is on trial.[2]

Had Professor Michalson lived until now, in all probability he would have written with greater urgency and even stronger rhetoric. The crisis in marriage and the integrity of the home in this country, and also in certain other parts of the world, has been compounded by many factors, not excepting the growing popular approbation for divorce, until the result, for concerned United Methodists and other Christians, is definitely one of baffled terror.

Christians, or, more broadly, people of a Judeo-Christian background, believe (some casually, others profoundly) that marriage is of God. Scriptural authority for this perspective is abundant and ranges from Psalm 68:6 to Mark 10:9, "What therefore God has joined together, let not man put asunder." There are a variety of additional passages in the Old Testament, the Gospels, Paul's Letters (particularly I Cor. 7), and the writings of John the Revelator. Perhaps the boldest and most memorable allusion is the classical reference to the marriage relation as suggestive of the kinship between Christ and his church to be found, among other places, in Ephesians 5.

One could marshal an impressive array of comments on the subject of Christian marriage by the great minds of the church, including Augustine, Kierkegaard, De Sales, Barth, Brunner, Bonhoeffer, C. S. Lewis, and others. An objective historian of human civilizations would have difficulty speaking adequately about the impact of the Judeo-Christian message on the solidarity of the home and family, including such collateral concerns as marriage, the sex relationship, monogamy, fidelity, parenthood, and the like.

Against the biblical and theological background there is the frightening profile of today's problem. Prenuptial agreements, for many, have assumed greater importance than religious covenants. Statistics on divorce and broken homes become gloomier as time goes by (perhaps now a staggering 50 percent), yet our familiarity with them seems to produce an increasingly cavalier acceptance of the sad facts. There is the added tragedy of the home that, while not broken, is chronically unhappy. Complex problems of child-rearing in a drug- and crime-ridden culture, the misunderstanding of sex and its failure to serve its intended purpose in marital stability, the dangers of an unbalanced budget and malignant debt, the steadily growing secularism of domestic life with its neglect of worship and prayer, soaring educational and medical costs, the uncertainty of the Social Security system, the inflated cost of housing for young families in particular, are formidable.

To quote Michalson again, "the wilting of the institution of marriage is significantly related to the flowering of secularism."[3] If he had lived, he might have added *affluence*.

Certainly the church, as well as the nation, has an enormous stake in the health of the institution of marriage and the family. Troubled young couples especially need understanding, support, and practical helpfulness from the people of God. If I were a pastor today, I would give this matter *primary priority* in my ministry and in programming for my congregation and constituency.

Let me offer some practical ideas at this point:

a. The church must accept certain things implicit in what we have called the sexual revolution, rather than undertake a massive and blindly puritanical resistance to *all* new perspectives. Exempted from such acceptance, for obvious reasons and in line with United Methodism's teachings, our Social

Principles, and the actions of General Conference, would be pornography, the legitimization of homosexual life-styles, and extramarital heterosexual practices. There are good books on this theme, including David R. Mace's *The Christian Response to the Sexual Revolution,* rev. ed. (Abingdon Press, 1987).

b. The church must undertake to know and understand the Christian position on the sacred and theological meanings of marriage and its related themes and to disseminate this knowledge effectively among its members and constituents. This can be done through preaching, Sunday school teaching, counseling, and family life conferences.

c. The church must articulate clearly and constantly its insistence on basic biblical standards where sexual and marital relations are concerned. It must not be afraid to take a stand counter to the trends of contemporary culture.

d. The church must continue to define defensible Christian positions and then vocalize them intelligently, on such critical issues as birth control, sex education, abortion, artificial insemination, divorce, racially mixed marriages, and genetic engineering.

e. The church must sharpen its skills in teaching youth and young adults its insights about sex, marriage, and the family. Much of our present problem derives from the church's frequent failure to teach effectively and urgently the groups most involved.

f. The church must offer healing love, forgiveness, and hope to all of those who have lost their way in modern life. The church is many things, but it is always and forever a shop where broken lives can be repaired. Canon T. Guy Rogers said a very significant word: "No one on behalf of the church ought to be allowed to handle the disagreements of married people who does not believe quite fervently in the power of conversion and the immediate influence of Christ on the lives of people today."

There is a lovely story of a young woman whose life had been broken on the reefs of moral error and who attended a communion service in a little kirk in the Scottish Highlands. When the invitation to join those at the Lord's table was given, she demurred. The minister, knowing her life, held forth the sacred elements to her and said gently, "Take it, lassie; it's for sinners!" The grace of the Lord Jesus Christ always is for sinners and also for those who are confused and in trouble.

g. The church, in a renewal of pastoral concern, must help families confront and solve the *many* problems they face, including childlessness, children with congenital handicaps, retardation, children in rebellion and caught in the drug and alcohol traps, teenage marriage, infidelity, chronic illness, terminal disease, tragedy, grief, marital discord, the presence of aged in-laws in the home, financial reverse, career collapse, and failing faith.

h. The church should magnify and interpret the *great* occasions of life such as birth, baptism, confirmation, marriage and death. In the holiest sense and in the light of the gospel's teachings, these are family festivals, either of joy or sorrow.

i. The church must seek for all family members, especially youth, the kind of experiential encounter with God that remains at the heart of our United Methodist interpretation of religion. As T. W. Manson said years ago, the teachings of the Christian religion are for *Kingdom people:* "The moral demands of Jesus presuppose a changed nature and disposition in man; they imply a previous conversion."[4]

No issue on the horizon should command more careful attention from the church than the current crisis in marriage and the home. Such careful attention, perhaps more than any other part of its ministry, will make the local church indispensable again in the life of its community.

6. *The life of the local church.* I have dealt elsewhere in this book specifically with the small membership church; I am speaking now about all churches. Sometimes I think United Methodism is dangerously close to going out of the local church business! I know that even in these pages I have included a paragraph affirming its importance and insisting that all connectional structures exist for its sake. I have no doubt that the leadership of the church would be in total agreement with this philosophy. What worries me is that our priorities and deeds often do not seem to support our theories.

Many of my district superintendents tell me that protests during charge conferences are becoming more regular and persistent. Searching questions are being asked and explanations sought. Why are the apportionments constantly going up? What does this program or that program really accomplish? How much is being spent on overhead and maintenance and even augmentation of institutional structure? Why are we asked to give so much additional money, and yet the church is losing members constantly? Will another General Conference mean larger connectional askings, and how can we pay these when our own membership is going down and we are sure to need a new roof and heating system in two years? What about our own annual conference structure, is it worth what it is costing us? And so the questions go on and on, and we try our best to provide honest and helpful answers. Some of our people, particularly those from other denominational backgrounds, cannot really seem to understand the information we are able to supply.

We call more meetings than we can even enumerate—on all levels. And our people come. Every Saturday at our headquarters building in Lakeland there are cars from all over the state of Florida. Many, but not all, of our meetings are important, but all of them are expensive! Our preachers stay so busy going to meeting of committees, subcommittees, boards, and agencies in our annual conferences and beyond that they must surely find their energy for parish work and preaching preparation severely dissipated and their time for their people critically curtailed.

If a bishop sometimes has the impression that the local church is existing more and more for the sake of the general church and its multifarious operations, how long will it be before this impression is abroad among our members to an extent that threatens the exchequer and the soul of connectionalism itself? These are serious questions in my mind that I believe should become subject matter for General Conferences.

Have we thought at all about what the farm crisis in our own country will mean to the health of the local church in those vast areas where, in the words of Vernon Schmid, "Farm families are slipping into despairing anonymity"? We were rightly concerned for a long time about the plight of migrant workers and other farm employees, but we may have come late as a church to anxiety for the survival of the farmers themselves. Again quoting Schmid:

> The nation's destiny may well be determined by how well it cares for the farmer. Such wounding of spirit does not enhance a people unless they respond with alacrity to the cries of wounded and broken hearts. There is little time for gamesmanship in congressional halls or White House think tanks; this crisis will not wait for rational political solutions. . . .
>
> Civilization may well feel the rumbling of destruction if it fails to reach out a healing hand to the people of the land.[5]

The great states of America's farm country traditionally have been strongholds of loyal United Methodism, and the local churches there are part of the backbone of our denomination and all of its benevolent activities. This is a matter of gravest concern for United Methodists everywhere, and especially for our leadership.

We finally enacted legislation focused more directly on the reality of the small church's administrative needs when we provided for the use of the Administrative Council instead of requiring such a church to supply a full complement of men, women, and youth for the larger organizational structure recommended by *The Book of Discipline*. This was a step in the right direction, but perhaps now we need to look honestly at revision and reduction of general church expenses (*not in mission but in organizational overhead and the cost of meetings*) so that the financial expectation from local churches will be more defensible and will enable the churches to provide needful parish and community programs and manage long-deferred plant maintenance. Perhaps a quadrennial emphasis, if there should be another one, ought to be about the local church, dramatizing its supreme significance in the life of our denomination. The Council of Bishops has already sensed the timeliness of revitalizing the life of individual congregations and is designing a major focus in this arena.

I, for one, believe it is time for us to turn our profession into practice, or we shall find ourselves one sad day looking upon a dead goose and no more golden eggs! We need to get back into the local church business!

7. *World Hunger.* Eighteen years ago the late great British author C. P. Snow wrote an apocalyptic warning which at that time was dismissed by most as unduly alarmist:

> Perhaps in ten years, millions of people in the poor countries are going to starve to death before our very eyes. . . . We shall see them doing so upon our television sets. How soon? How many deaths? Can they be prevented? Can they be minimized? Those are the most important questions in our world today.[6]

At the time Mr. Snow offered his prediction the experts were relying on miracle seeds and fertilizers to create a global "green revolution" and were even projecting self-sufficiency in food supplies for such chronically hungry nations as India. A major role to be played by the sea in solving the world's food problems was being anticipated, but the scene has shifted today. Water pollution has destroyed much of the fish life on the world's continental shelves. Fertilizer, in many places, has become prohibitively expensive. Industrial nations have continued to buy up the dwindling supplies of food and so have driven food prices higher than poorer countries can afford to pay. Future prospects are threatened by the old Malthusian specter of population explosion.

Some of us sat for two hours with United States Ambassador Thomas to the Republic of Kenya when the World Methodist Conference met in Nairobi in the summer of 1986. I asked the ambassador what he regarded as Kenya's principal problem. His reply was instant: "Population control." He explained how the number of people in Nairobi had trebled in a handful of years. The population of the entire country, he said, had now reached twenty million. The ambassador reported sadly how Roman Catholic beliefs concerning birth control continue to hamper the efforts of an enlightened government to teach its families the dangers of a burgeoning population in a land not yet prepared to deal adequately with food supplies, housing, and the expense of medical care and education. It is quite obvious that the Republic of Kenya with its beloved president and friendly, gracious citizens is in a more fortunate position to guard its future than some of the new nations in Africa, but its present needs are still very critical.

We are familiar with the starvation tragedy in Ethiopia, and the continuing threat of famine perennially present in several sub-Sahara African nations—and always in India. At least half of the world's total population, we are told, live in perpetual hunger. The crisis of the American farms could complicate the situation greatly.

Surely Jesus' own teaching about our fundamental duty to feed those who are hungry is still basic in any understanding of his gospel. The work of UMCOR in our own United Methodism, complemented by other organizations such as Church World Service (a ministry of the National Council of the Churches of Christ) and Bread for the World, has engendered enthusiastic support from United Methodist people. Their record of giving to relieve world hunger is one of the exciting chapters in the story of philanthropy. The need in future years will be extravagantly greater than past or present challenges—one strong argument in favor of a simpler life-style among our United Methodist people which would enable us to share more generously with those who are less fortunate than we are. In addition, through the worldwide mission and influence of United Methodism and the ecumenical church, constant efforts must be made to educate the people of developing nations, and other countries as well, in effective production, conservation, and distribution of foodstuffs. Always a strong Christian witness must be offered to the governments of the world with their different economic structures, encouraging them to identify the root causes behind human hunger and to set about alleviating and removing them. United Methodism will never be more Christlike in its ministry than when it addresses this problem of world hunger.

8. *The Sunday school.* When we allowed the Sunday school to go down, we invoked the era of greatest membership loss in The United Methodist Church. We ought to have known better, for the Sunday school has always been our most dependable evangelistic arm. Historically it has proved to be the surest of all channels for guiding men, women, boys, and girls into Christian commitment and church membership. I do not believe that our membership losses will ever be reversed until we have reinstated a vital Sunday school program,

designed for these times and dedicated to that kind of teaching of the Word of God by committed Christians that, under the guidance of the Holy Spirit, is bound to produce disciples. Let us pray that the spirit of Robert Raikes, the British philanthropist and newspaper publisher who began the Sunday school movement, may anoint United Methodism with imaginative zeal sufficient to revive and refashion this mighty enterprise of mind and soul in our denomination. Nothing could be more therapeutic for the health of The United Methodist Church.

9. *The crisis of thought.*[7] John Naisbitt, in *Megatrends*,[8] helped familiarize contemporary Americans with the exciting reality of change, possibly the only constant in a world of variables today. He talked at length about decentralization, mass media, multiple-option society, "high-tech/high-touch" (the reaction against "anti-human" gadgetry), individualism, globalism, and the reconceptualization of education. He was far more optimistic than many other futurists speaking to our generation.

In 1974 the Club of Rome (an elite organization of international scientists and economists) published a sobering book entitled *The Limits of Growth,* attempting to establish the fact that the world is running out of everything except people and speaking of the diminishing amount of arable land, the danger of continuing population explosion, the exhaustion within one hundred years of many non-renewable resources, and the sure collapse of the industrial age.

The late R. Buckminster Fuller, inventor and thinker, denying the second law of thermodynamics, taught that life and knowledge will prove anti-entropic and that the human family will survive by doing more and more with less and less. He too envisioned a *post-industrial age* based on intellectual, cultural, and moral growth.

Social critic Alvin Toffler in *The Third Wave* undertakes to analyze the industrial urban society which developed in the West two centuries ago, following the rural and agricultural age, declaring that this was responsible for the growth of nationalism and patriotism as opposed to loyalty to a world community, and that this society used the cheap labor and materials available from undeveloped nations to supply its operations. He believes that post-industrial technology will catapult civilization into a new age, the Age of Information, which he identifies as the *"third wave."*[9]

As all of us know, the incredible magic of computer science is already revolutionizing business, industry, education, and government, and also strongly if not radically affecting the church.

The revolutionary implications of the new physics for religious thinking will surely prove to be one of the most important frontiers for theologians and religious philosophers in the years just ahead. The mysteries of quantum theory with its bewildering effort to explain a multitude of heretofore baffling phenomena associated with various scientific processes have helped produce the laser, the semiconductor, the superconductor, the electron microscope, and nuclear power. A basic issue raised by quantum theory is whether or not any universe at all truly exists independent of the observer. The reality or unreality of subatomic particles intimidates many Christians who forget that Scripture affirms for nature a divinely given and perpetuated life of its own, quite apart from that of human beings.

Added to the complexities of the crisis in thought already mentioned are the problems posed by *biotechnology*. Prominent is the issue of genetic engineering, a science based on the discovery of the shape of the DNA molecule and capable of altering the normal functions of cell replication. Experimentation in this delicate but radical area has been going on now for more than fifteen years. Actually, we are told, it may harbor positive as well as negative possibilities for the human family. Here is a fresh, unprecedented challenge to the Christian mind, for the ultimate results of such scientific findings may be influenced and even determined by the impact of the gospel's ethical teachings.

When one studies the implications of the contemporary crisis in thought, a fact of our present life neither deniable nor reversible, he or she would do well to read and ponder *The Other Side of 1984,* the Newbigin book to which I refer often in these chapters, and to use its careful historical review of the post-Enlightenment era as a background for assessing the effects that may be expected from these scientific miracles and their meanings for the church and its mission. Newbigin, of course, believes that scientific influence on human action and destiny will have a limited lifetime.

Perhaps, in the long run, the most critical of all the real issues confronting United Methodism today will prove to be both its immediate and long-range reaction to this complex crisis in human thought. Christian faith solidly based on the Bible and informed by sound theology is more than equal to the colossal challenge posed by the new science. Indeed, the preservation of civilization itself demands the intercession of a church knowledgeable, faith-filled, and Spirit-led.

No church served and guided by ministers unwilling to study and master the complicated signs of the times in this crisis of thought can hope to survive far beyond the end of this century, nor is United Methodist survival probable if we should ignore an issue so vital and sweeping as this one.

10. *Church growth.* I want United Methodism to grow because I am convinced that its rich legacy of religious understanding is important for the ecumenical church and for the confused age in which we are called on to be His witnesses. However, I am not interested primarily in numbers—not even the 20,000,000 members foreseen by 1992. I have never believed we had as many members as we claimed, for I know (and probably used to practice!) the careless arithmetic for which preachers are often notorious. Much of the loss recorded across recent years constitutes the elimination of numbers who were never there and represents no real diminution in denominational strength. I am far more interested in developing discipleship and in winning human beings to the Christian life by *genuine* conversion or reclamation. Although this may sound heretical, I can envision the possibility of our having a far stronger United Methodism with 7,000,000 people than 9,000,000 provided they are committed and active.

Nor do I wish to foster church growth by urging superficial, merely popular preaching that avoids the real and hard questions of life and religion, or by taking the public pulse and then prescribing church stances and programs designed for accommodation to a contemporary but apostate culture. I am not impressed by the spectacular evangelists who capture headlines by their promotion of moral majorities, and I do not wish the United Methodism I love to become in our time simply an overgrown fundamentalist cult. I love my country dearly, but I do not believe in a civil religion. We have our own precious heritage, richer in content and promise than we have ever dreamed, and we must keep it pure and powerful in our time or we shall fail both God and the human family.

Of course I believe in evangelism. My whole life as a minister has sought to sound its authentic note. I believe in church growth and church extension. I long for our preachers to proclaim the gospel so relevantly and thrillingly that throngs will crowd our churches Sunday after Sunday. I want United Methodism to meet the needs and help solve the problems of people who live and struggle today, but I want us to be true to our great underlying principles and never surrender to gimmicks and shortcuts that prostitute the holy meaning of the Christian gospel and the Wesleyan tradition. That is too high a price to pay for statistical glory.

I do deeply believe that our church *can* grow in the right way if you and I are willing to pay the price, and with God's help!

A Final Word for This Chapter

Many issues have not been mentioned, including the mortal menace of the drug culture with *crack cocaine* as one of its latest complications, the sickness of pornography, our unresolved differences about ministry and ordination, and the shockingly low trust level existing between the laity and the administrative structures of the church—and perhaps the other way around as well. The *general spiritual malaise* of our church, my major concern, is actually the theme running through all the pages of this volume.

Bishop Short was right. It's a long way from the time when our people argued about women bobbing their hair!

CHAPTER NINE

If Morning Is to Come

Dare we believe in the future of The United Methodist Church as a vital part of God's plan for the redemption of his world?

This is a serious query, not just a rhetorical question that some one of us might ask at the beginning of a Sunday morning sermon, and then attempt to answer in a conventional manner. There is no doubt about it; for many the present statistics of annual loss oppose an affirmative answer to this query. Too, the image of our church, once resplendent with all the glory of the Wesleyan legacy, has been tarnished currently by the ruthless attacks of a secular world and a secular press seemingly determined to find United Methodism's jugular vein and inflict crippling if not mortal injury. Then there are problems of our own which, up until now, we have appeared afraid to confront honestly, or, attempting to confront them, have foundered awkwardly in our efforts to set our house in order.

Twenty years ago Dean Fitch spoke of "the idolatry of secularism."[1] His words still serve to explain the fundamental *Protestant sickness* to which he alluded at that time.

How do we who are United Methodists, clerical and lay, penetrate the hard crust that envelops the mind and heart of a modern human being, and so gain the attention of that person for the Christian gospel? He or she needs *something* desperately—and knows as much. Often, to recall the language in II Timothy 3:5, the form of religion has become so familiar and cold that its power seems, to hardened, weary people in the 1980s, unreal and difficult for the materialistic mind to accept. Thus the contemporary person usually does not take it seriously.

Many typical individuals in our times are not really interested in organized religion, but they are still susceptible to Jesus Christ, enamored of that strange Man upon a cross. When the right words are spoken, they are ready to ask him their hard questions and to hear his answers.

This is the church's task in our generation: to learn how to speak the right words, to lift Jesus Christ out of his institutional sepulcher so that he may become a living Savior for a hurting, frightened, cynical age.

Someone long ago said that every important reality known to humans begins as an experience, becomes an idea, next a doctrine, then a dogma, and finally an institution. When the church was young, it was still closely related to the rapture of the New Testament *experience.* Now, centuries later in the Western world at least, it has passed through a long and persistent hardening process that has destroyed much of its freshness, vitality, and vigor. Becoming rich in the possessions of this world, it has lost the depth of its spiritual power somewhere across the years. There is frightening simplicity in our challenge; we must find a way to turn morning light upon the deep darkness of an overorganized institution.

It can be done, if we are willing as a church to criticize ourselves and address our problems and if in the process we are able to recapture the springtime of our own faith.

Therefore, my answer to the question I raised in the opening sentence of this chapter is a *resounding yes*—provided the leaders of our church, clergy and lay, are prepared to do certain things.

1. *We must recognize the terrible urgency of our situation.* United Methodists are confronted in these times by their greatest opportunity—and perhaps their final one.

Let me put it in a story. Many years ago there was a woman in Chicago whose child was desperately ill and who read in the papers that the great Austrian orthopedic surgeon, Dr. Adolf Lorenz, was in the city. In desperate faith she prayed that God would send the renowned specialist into her modest home to cure her child. There was no influence to summon him, no money to pay him—only her prayer. In the midst of a busy day, Dr. Lorenz went out to relax and to see the remoter sections of that vast city by the lake. He told his driver as they came to a humble residential area to let him out for an hour's stroll and to pick him up at a designated place. In the midst of his walk a sudden violent rainstorm swept down over Chicago and the stranded doctor sought brief shelter in a simple cottage near where he was walking—the very house, it happened, where the praying mother and the sick child lived. But when he courteously gave his last name and asked for sanctuary from the rain, he was rudely and curtly refused admission. The next morning the Chicago papers carried the famous doctor's indignant account of a poor housewife's inhospitality to a man from another land seeking shelter from a storm. And in the home where it all happened, a shocked and incredulous woman, the woman who had not really expected God to send Adolf Lorenz, was overcome by sorrow and remorse because she had missed the opportunity that God had provided.

In a world stunned by tragedy and made brittle and cynical by its own pagan pantheon, may God forbid that anyone of us should fail to comprehend the ultimacy of the spiritual crisis into which our world is plunged and the relationship of our own church to that crisis. In other times it was necessary for God to turn away from the people upon whom he had been accustomed to depend and to raise up other agents for his use. It could happen again. There are signs that the slumbering giant which is The United Methodist Church is beginning to stir, hopeful signs, but *now* is the urgent moment for action. It is doubtful that the opportunity will come again in our time.

2. *We must review our resources.* Sometimes even those of us who are in leadership positions in the church are so close to the rich ingredients of our heritage that we take their presence and power for granted.

a. The greatest of our resources, apart from the Bible itself and the treasury of Christian doctrines belonging to the whole family of God, is *the legacy that John Wesley bequeathed to his followers.* The England of Wesley's day was sick unto death with what appeared to be incurable moral and spiritual maladies—not unlike the America of these closing years of the twentieth century. The Wesleyan Revival made a frontal attack upon the massive unrighteousness that held England and its churches in its grip. As Wesley undertook to restore morality and decency to Britain, he dared to expose ungodliness in places both high and low. On August 24, 1744, he preached in St. Mary's Church in Oxford, before a university congregation, his famous sermon "Scriptural Christianity," asking his congregation these questions: "Where does this Christianity now exist? Where, I pray, do the Christians live? Is this city a Christian city? Is Christianity, Scriptural Christianity, found here? Are we, considered as a community of men, so 'filled with the Holy Ghost' as to enjoy in our hearts and show forth in our lives the genuine fruits of that Spirit?"[2]

In this celebrated message, John Wesley suggested to his hearers at St. Mary's that living clean and wholesome lives could be vastly more important than dialoguing about theology, suggesting that Christians must become "lively portraitures of Him whom ye are appointed to represent among men."[3] The transformation that the ministry and preaching of the Wesley brothers wrought in old England was the most startling miracle of the eighteenth century, an event that the French historian Elie Halévy was later to describe as being important enough to save England from the serious possibility of a disaster as colossal as the French Revolution.[4]

The example of the Wesleys in their time ought to be reproducible by their followers in today's world where moral decay is far more pervasive than it was in eighteenth-century England with its rationalism and deism. This is the torch that has been handed to us. Often in recent years we have allowed other denominations, some of them newer and smaller than ours, to appropriate our theological and spiritual properties. Many of these churches are growing solidly and steadily as a result, and, if we are honest, are blessing America in an era of uncontrolled crime and violence. We must learn again how to make our own pulpits ring with the message of John Wesley's vibrant understanding of the Christian faith, giving his doctrines and his courageous moral pronouncements to the people of our time. For reasons always beyond our full understanding, God has been pleased to use this message in the past, and he will use it again.

Also a part of Wesley's legacy is our church's *incomparable organization*. John Wesley was a structural genius. The relatively simple but magnificent design of United Methodism is able to support with disarming ease a far-flung practical but imaginative program of Christian mission, more comprehensive and effective than any other in the entire community of faith with the possible exception of that presided over by the Roman Catholic Church. Our organization often is the marvel not only of the religious world but also of the secular world as well. However, as this book has sought to remind us, definite caution always must be exercised to avoid unnecessary proliferation of structure at the expense of the local church.

b. Also of significance as resources are *our system of church law and our carefully crafted statements of theological and ethical conviction.* Some of this we owe to those who lived long before us, but some is the result of the thoughtful, often heated deliberations of our General Conferences, themselves among the most dramatic experiments in working democracy the church world (and perhaps the secular world as well) has ever known. We have a solid foundation upon which to rest both our polity and program as a denomination.

c. Less measurable as an asset but perhaps of even greater importance is the *present expectant, wistful mood of our people*—quite apparent to any of us in close relationship to grass-roots United Methodism. In spite of the disturbances and dangers to which this book has made reference, there is a massive spiritual hunger in the hearts of our people and in the world's heart at this moment in human history. In the picturesque language of II Samuel 5:24, which preachers of another day invoked in their revival messages, there is "the sound of marching in the tops of the balsam trees." As has happened again and again across the Christian centuries, the apparent hopelessness of the human situation is providing fertile soil in which to plant the seeds of Christian faith. Our theology and organization, informed by the sense of evangelical urgency that has always been present in the Methodist tradition, are ideally suited to today's circumstances and needs. The time is propitious for a renaissance of belief, a reawakening of spiritual power in our denomination.

3. *We must face our problems with honest realism.* Committee action, task forces, and convocations will not do the job. Our

situation requires a consuming consciousness in the mind and soul of our church that we are confronted with an unprecedented opportunity, an opportunity presently neutralized by our spiritual condition. All of our false pride, our logical rationalization, our lively instinct for institutional self-preservation, our bitter impulse to silence our critics, and the malignancy of our affluent apathy must be driven from our minds and hearts. We must be able to look at every problem with fresh vision and try with desperate intensity to understand why we have lost our influence and impact upon this age—something far more significant than mere numbers.

We may not be able to bring ourselves to do this. However, if it is not done, the vigorous, vital spiritual entity that has been our church in other years will not come to life again in our time. There will be some kind of United Methodist Church, to be sure, and its dignified facade probably will continue to conceal its inner decay, at least until a new century has begun. But the kind of life that the early Methodist movement, including the rich heritage of the Church of the United Brethren in Christ and the Evangelical Church, breathed into communities and social structures when our three denominations were young, will remain but a lovely memory in history. Let there be no misunderstanding at this point: I am speaking of the *real* problems of United Methodism, and not of membership loss which is but a symptom of far deeper troubles. I am aware also that, for the time being at least, we must continue to wrestle with the issue of our very *bigness,* which can make even precious commodities like renewal and revival unmanageable. This is something with which we have to live, and our acknowledgment of its difficulty will be helpful in itself. What I am calling for here, on the part of each of us, is a full measure of raw, uncompromising candor until we are able *to see the picture as it really is,* and as many of our own members and more outside our church already see it.

4. We must decide whether or not *we are ready to pay the price involved in solving our problems.* Many of us in leadership positions have become loyal and comfortable "company" people. In our present condition we are incapable of applying the kind of *tough love* that the situation demands. The question

confronting us is simple and basic, Will we make that revolutionary adjustment in our own perspectives that can begin the entire process of change and, if you will, redemption throughout United Methodism and particularly in this country? This book has alluded to many specific problems as one deeply concerned person sees them. It has not always offered precise answers, but these will be forthcoming when the attitudes of our own minds and hearts are made right. The question is, Are we prepared to make them right?

5. *We must believe the gospel and give ourselves anew to its power.* Our secular age dons the livery of the spiritual as awkwardly as a modern novelist would put on the prose of a Bunyan or a Dickens. The raucous noises of today's punk rock culture drown out the quiet loveliness of a Beethoven sonata or a Schubert symphony. It is a time of rationalized hedonism and arrogant doubt with a backdrop of liberty turned into license and tradition and convention broken into a million fragments.

But over against all of this, we have the *wonder of the gospel* with its timeless power to "save unto the uttermost" both individuals and human society whenever it is given opportunity. That gospel is inexhaustible.

Arthur John Gossip used to remind young ministers that the Christian faith is not a little pond around which they may stroll for half an hour and then say, "There it is, you see," but that it is instead a tremendous shoreless sea, reaching far beyond our poor human capacity ever to search it all out. The resurrection of Christ, upon which everything of faith finally rests, was itself, in the vivid simile of European theologian Karl Heim, like the collapse of a dike in the low countries on the shores of the North Sea. Even if it were but one little section, an event of small significance in itself, one is aware that its consequences are *beyond calculation,* for beyond the dike surges the tumultuous sea which will burst through the opening. This is what Paul knew when he declared, after he had seen the risen Savior, "Christ [is] . . . the first fruits of those who have fallen asleep" (I Cor. 15:20). All meaning of our faith revolves around an individual relationship that each of us has with God—the God of the resurrected Savior.

The relevant question is this one, Do you and I have such a

relationship, and is it alive and contemporary? We so often live in spiritual poverty when the very bounty of heaven is ours for the taking. We enter with such hesitancy into the mystery and glory of the Christian promises, and thus fail to appropriate the limitless power that our Lord has placed at the disposal of those who believe in him.

What I am trying to say is that the traditional energy of Christian experience as John Wesley described and interpreted it needs to lay fresh hold upon people like you and me until, knowing Jesus Christ in his wonder-working power, we are able to realize again that the church, even our church, is of God. Then, with the help of the Holy Spirit, we can do our human best with a sure confidence that God himself will perfect our imperfections and complete our task.

In practical language, all of this means ruthless scrutiny of one's own spiritual condition, a deliberate searching of the Scriptures under the Holy Spirit's tutelage, experiential recovery of prevailing prayer's deep, throbbing meanings, and a total fresh surrender of one's life to the gospel's revolutionary power until the ancient drama of salvation and sanctification is played out again in the theaters of our souls. It is the reenactment of revival, spiritual recrudescence, the glory of new birth until each of us becomes again a "new creature" in Christ. The form of religion to which we have clung for so long will be *baptized with fire* from heaven itself. For the average United Methodist layperson or minister, this is *serious business!*

We may take all the other steps I have listed in this chapter but until we take this final one, morning cannot come.

・・・

The words I have written for my readers I have written for myself as well. Whatever the problems of The United Methodist Church, I am a part of them. If I love my church as much as I think I do, I shall be willing to be used to discover and accomplish their solutions. If I know my own heart, and if I correctly assess the hearts of my fellow United Methodists in this disturbed hour, I deeply believe that enough of us, indeed, are ready to pay the price involved in recovering the spiritual greatness of United Methodism for God to make it happen.

Some years ago my wife and I attended a semiannual meeting of the Council of Bishops in Washington, D.C. The business sessions were laden with heavy and often dismal matters: a strike in Pikesville, Kentucky; the terrors of floods, earthquakes, hurricanes; the awful implications for the church in the tragedy of Watergate. Then, on Thursday night, the Thursday night after Easter, as guests of Bishop and Mrs. W. Earl Ledden, we all went to the fabulous Kennedy Center for the Performing Arts and listened to the National Symphony Orchestra play Gustav Mahler's Second Symphony, the "Resurrection Symphony." I think I have never heard such magnificent music. The triumphant message of the risen Christ broke through the stirring measures of the symphony with surpassing power. It was an overwhelming experience and I have recalled it many, many times in the years since.

So it is that, for the Christian, the gloom and despair of life's burdens and issues are suddenly shattered by the crashing chords of resurrection truth and promise. The darkness of the night is flooded with unearthly light. Our faith is secure in the risen Redeemer. I still like Herbert Butterfield's words about facing the future: "Hold to Christ, and for the rest be totally uncommitted." As I close this volume, my confidence, and I hope yours as well, is in the resurection faith, to which I witness gratefully and gladly before the world.

My heart is *filled with hope* for The United Methodist Church in the tomorrows that lie ahead. Morning will come.

NOTES

Introduction

1. William H. Willimon, in an address given in Nashville, Tennessee, on September 5, 1986, and reported by *United Methodist Communications* on September 8, 1986, in a release by Thomas S. McAnally.
2. Earl G. Hunt, Jr., *I Have Believed: A Bishop Talks About His Faith* (Nashville: The Upper Room, 1980).
3. "The Constitution," Paragraph 50, Article III, supported by "The Superintendency," Paragraph 514, Section IV, "Specific Responsibilities of Bishops," in *The Book of Discipline of The United Methodist Church, 1984* (Nashville: The United Methodist Publishing House, 1984), pp. 34, 261-62.
4. Gilbert Keith Chesterton, *As I Was Saying: A Chesterton Reader*, ed. Robert Knille (Grand Rapids: Wm. B. Eerdmans Publishing Co., 1985), pp. 3, 183.

Chapter One

1. Lesslie Newbigin, *The Good Shepherd*, American ed. (Grand Rapids: Wm. B. Eerdmans Publishing Co., 1977), p. 12.
2. Clarence Edward Macartney in a sermon delivered at First Methodist Church, Morristown, Tennessee, autumn, 1955.
3. Lesslie Newbigin, *The Other Side of 1984: Questions for the Churches* (Geneva: World Council of Churches, 1983). Obtainable in the U.S.A. from the Division of Overseas Ministries of the National Council of the Churches of Christ.
4. Richard B. Wilke, *And Are We Yet Alive?* (Nashville: Abingdon Press, 1986).
5. Alan K. Waltz, *Images of the Future, Into Our Third Century* series, ed. Ezra Earl Jones (Nashville: Abingdon Press, 1980), pp. 27, 28.
6. Ibid., p. 29.
7. The word *historic* is used here and in some other places in this book to differentiate between those evangelical convictions that belong to the main sweep of Christian history and certain limited uses of the adjective "evangelical" current in recent years to describe the conservative (sometimes reactionary) contingent of the Christian community.
8. Albert C. Outler, "What's Ahead for the Church?" *World Outlook*, April, 1969.
9. Hunt, *I Have Believed*, chapter 3, pp. 61-63.
10. Dean J. Snyder, "Confessions of a Closet Charismatic," *The Christian Century*, October 5, 1983.
11. Warren J. Hartman, *Discipleship Trends* (General Board of Discipleship of The United Methodist Church, August, 1986), p. 1.
12. Thomas S. Kepler, *Leaves from a Spiritual Notebook* (Nashville: Abingdon Press, 1960), p. 250.

13. Samuel H. Miller, *Man the Believer* (Nashville: Abingdon Press, 1968), p. 125.
14. "The Order for Confirmation and Reception into the Church," *Ritual of The United Methodist Church* (Nashville: The United Methodist Publishing House, 1964), p. 16.

Chapter Two

1. D. Elton Trueblood, *The Essence of Spiritual Religion* (New York: Harper & Row, 1975), p. 138.
2. John R. Mott, *Liberating the Lay Forces of Christianity* (New York: Macmillan, 1932).
3. M. L. Brownsberger, "From the Other Side of the Pulpit," *The Christian Century*, August 27–September 3, 1986. This ordained Presbyterian minister and corporate executive offers some provocative thoughts: "During the ten years that I have been in business, I have yet to hear a sermon or read a theologian that helps me affirm what I do as a Christian in the American political economy." He goes on to comment that American preaching was influenced for years by German reformed theology, but now resonates to Latin American liberation theology and permits the agenda of the Christian pulpit to be set by "the experience of a particular class of people under particular political conditions" so that "the 'character' of American life is exposed as being 'really' composed of alienation, greed, avarice, inequality, creedal chaos, exploitation, injustice, selfishness, economic . . . colonialism." He acknowledges that "there are manifestations of evil in American economic, political and religious life," but argues that our unique experience calls for "an equally unique approach to theology" instead of careless appropriation of the kind of approach that seems relevant somewhere else in the world but may not belong here. This is heady stuff for the contemporary liberal United Methodist leadership mind, but surely worthy of thought and honest dialogue.
4. Mott, *Liberating the Lay Forces of Christianity*, p. 43.
5. From "Meditation XVII" in *Devotions upon Emergent Occasions*.

Chapter Three

1. George M. Docherty, *One Way of Living* (New York: Harper & Brothers, 1958), pp. 3-19. A composite of several related statements in this chapter.
2. Ruth Truman, *Underground Manual for Ministers' Wives* (Nashville: Abingdon Press, 1974). Out of print.
3. Arthur Wentworth Hewitt, *The Old Brick Manse* (New York: Harper & Row, 1966).
4. Gerald F. Kennedy, *God's God News: The Lyman Beecher Lectures at Yale* (New York: Harper & Brothers, 1955), p. 114.
5. William L. Stidger, "Mine the Mighty Ordination," in *The Varieties of Present-day Preaching*, ed. G. Bromley Oxnam (New York: Abingdon Press, 1932), p. 20. Words are part of a passage taken from Edward S. Minde's book *George Whitefield*, but their actual author is not named.

Chapter Four

1. Carl F. H. Henry, "Liberation Theology and the Scriptures," in *Liberation Theology*, ed. Ronald Nash (Milford, Mich.: Mott Media, 1984), p. 194.

NOTES

2. Colin W. Williams, *John Wesley's Theology Today* (Nashville: Abingdon Press, 1960).
3. Robert E. Fitch, "The Protestant Sickness," *Religion in Life*, vol. 35, Fall, 1966, pp. 498-505.
4. William Barclay, *Introducing the Bible* (Nashville: Abingdon Press, 1972), p. 147.
5. *The Works of the Reverend John Wesley, A.M.*, vol. I (New York: B. Waugh & T. Mason, 1835), p. xix.
6. Mack B. Stokes, *The Bible in the Wesleyan Heritage* (Nashville: Abingdon Press, 1979), p. 16.
7. Martin Marty, *The Public Church* (New York: Crossword Publishing Company, 1981), p. 169.
8. José M. Bonino, *Doing Theology in a Revolutionary Situation*, ed. William H. Lazareth (Philadelphia: Fortress Press, 1975), p. 47.
9. William Allen White, editor of *Emporia Gazette*, letter to author, January 22, 1941.

Chapter Five

1. Kenneth Scott Latourette, *Beyond the Ranges* (Grand Rapids: Wm. B. Eerdmans Publishing Co., 1967), p. 5. This is an allusion to Rudyard Kipling's poem "The Explorer," as is the book's title.
2. Leslie D. Weatherhead, *Time for God* (Nashville: Abingdon Press, 1967), p. 137.
3. Karl Barth, *Call for God*, trans. A. T. Mackay (New York: Harper & Row, 1967).
4. Emil Brunner, *I Believe in the Living God*, trans. and ed. John Holden (Philadelphia: Westminster Press, 1961).
5. Reinhold Niebuhr, *Justice and Mercy*, ed. Ursula M. Niebuhr (New York: Harper & Row, 1974).
6. Nels F. S. Ferré, *The Extreme Center* (Waco: Word Books, 1973).
7. David H. C. Read, *Sent from God* (Nashville: Abingdon Press, 1974), p. 30.
8. Harold Cooke Phillips, *Bearing Witness to the Truth* (New York: Abingdon-Cokesbury, 1949).
9. Richard Eslinger, *A New Hearing: Living Options in Homiletic Method* (Nashville: Abingdon Press, 1987).
10. Eugene L. Lowry, *Doing Time in the Pulpit* (Nashville: Abingdon Press, 1985).
11. Edmund A. Steimle, et al., *Preaching the Story* (Philadelphia: Fortress Press, 1980).
12. Frederick Buechner, *Telling the Truth* (New York: Harper & Row, 1977).
13. Read, *Sent from God*.
14. D. T. Niles, *The Preacher's Task and the Stone of Stumbling*, 1957 Lyman Beecher Lectures (New York: Harper & Brothers, 1958), p. 112.
15. Helmut Thielicke, *The Trouble with the Church*, trans. and ed. John W. Doberstein (New York: Harper & Row, 1965), p. 1.

Chapter Six

1. Joe A. Howell and Daniel Eidson, *The Idea of an Ideal Liberal Arts College* (Lanham, Md.: University Press of America, 1985).

Chapter Seven

1. William B. Lawrence, "Ralph Sockman: The Compleat Methodist," *Quarterly Review, A Scholarly Journal for Reflection on Ministry,* Winter, 1985.
2. Francis Gerald Ensley, *John Wesley, Evangelist* (Nashville: Methodist Evangelistic Materials, 1958), p. 46.
3. Charles W. Ferguson, *Organizing to Beat the Devil* (New York: Doubleday & Company, 1971), pp. vii-viii.
4. Jack M. Tuell, *The Organization of The United Methodist Church,* rev. ed. (Nashville: Abingdon Press, 1985), p. 8.
5. *Daily Christian Advocate,* May 7, 1984, Calendar #0329, p. 48.
6. Bishop William R. Cannon, Episcopal Address to the 1984 General Conference, *Daily Christian Advocate,* May 2, 1984, p. 17.
7. Lesslie Newbigin, *Foolishness to the Greeks: The Gospel and Western Culture* (Grand Rapids: Wm. B. Eerdmans Publishing Co., 1986). Dr. Newbigin offers in this provocative work strong critiques both of capitalism and socialism, suggesting that Christians must in the end offer a more biblical alternative to both.
8. Tom H. Matheny, "Reforming Episcopal Elections," *Circuit Rider,* February, 1983, pp. 15-16.
9. Henri J. M. Nouwen, *The Wounded Healer* (New York: Doubleday & Co., 1972), pp. 36-46.
10. Ibid., p. 37.

Chapter Eight

1. Jonathan Schell, *The Fate of the Earth* (New York: Alfred Knopf, 1982.)
2. Carl Michalson, *Faith for Personal Crisis* (New York: Charles Scribner Sons, 1958), p. 114.
3. Ibid., 115.
4. T. W. Manson, *The Teachings of Jesus* (Cambridge: Cambridge University Press, 1963), p. 299.
5. Vernon Schmid, "The Summer of Our Sorrow," *The Christian Century,* December 4, 1985.
6. C. P. Snow, quoted in "Running Out of Food?" *Newsweek,* April 1, 1974, p. 40.
7. In addition to the books referred to I am indebted for certain ideas in this section to Professor Richard Lovelace of Gordon-Conwell Theological Seminary, my casual but respected friend, who wrote "Future Shock and Christian Hope," *Christianity Today,* August 5, 1983, pp. 12-16.
8. John Naisbitt, *Megatrends* (New York: Warner Books, 1983).
9. Alvin Toffler, *The Third Wave* (New York: Telecom Library, 1980).

Chapter Nine

1. Fitch, "The Protestant Sickness."
2. John Wesley, *The Works of John Wesley,* vol. I, ed. Albert C. Outler (Nashville: Abingdon Press, 1984), p. 174.

NOTES

3. Ibid., p. 175. Also quoted, with helpful comments, in William R. Cannon, *The Theology of John Wesley* (Nashville: Abingdon-Cokesbury Press, 1946), p. 25.
4. Elie Halévy, *The Birth of Methodism in England,* 5 vols. (Chicago: The University of Chicago Press, 1971), pp. 1, 70.

My Weirdtastic School #7

Mr. and Mrs. Phelps Need Some Help!

Dan Gutman

Pictures by
Jim Paillot

HARPER
An Imprint of HarperCollinsPublishers

To James Campbell

Special thanks to Sheila Creaser, Brandi Eilean,
Kathleen Guinnane, Christa Kozoriz-Hendy,
Valerey Hess, Lauri Harvey Keagle, Bob Laven,
Becky Wharton-Liechti, Dana Mesh, Kim O'Brien,
Kelly Reyome Rardin, Karen Sweetwood Roth,
Amy Weaver Sadler, Tricia Windy Woodward

My Weirdtastic School #7: Mr. and Mrs. Phelps Need Some Help!
Text copyright © 2025 by Dan Gutman
Illustrations copyright © 2025 by Jim Paillot
All rights reserved. Manufactured in Crawfordsville, IN, United State of America.
No part of this book may be used or reproduced in any manner whatsoever without
written permission except in the case of brief quotations embodied in critical
articles and reviews. For information address HarperCollins Children's Books,
a division of HarperCollins Publishers, 195 Broadway, New York, NY 10007.
www.harpercollinschildrens.com

Library of Congress Control Number: 2024942798
ISBN 978-0-06-337387-7 (pbk bdg) — ISBN 978-0-06-337388-4 (trade bdg)

Typography by Laura Mock
24 25 26 27 28 LBC 5 4 3 2 1

First Edition

Contents

1. How Do They Get Jelly Out of Jellyfish?   1
2. Meet the Phelpses   9
3. Dad Puts Me to Sleep   20
4. Measure Twice, Cut Once   28
5. Snickerdoodles   38
6. Racecar Backward   51
7. Baking Baguettes   59
8. Crying   69
9. The Last Straw   76
10. Choose Your Weapons   85
11. Duels Are Cool   93

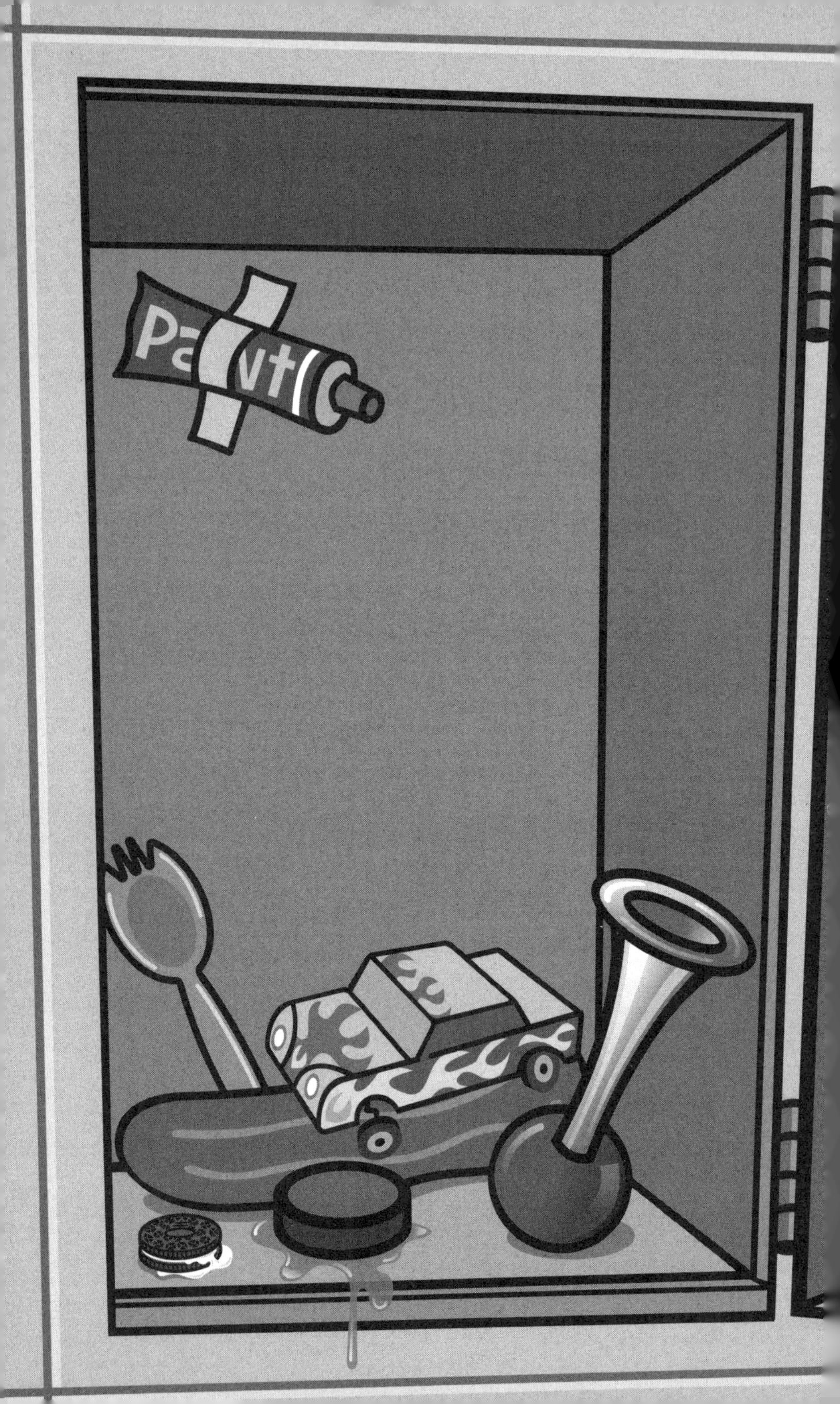

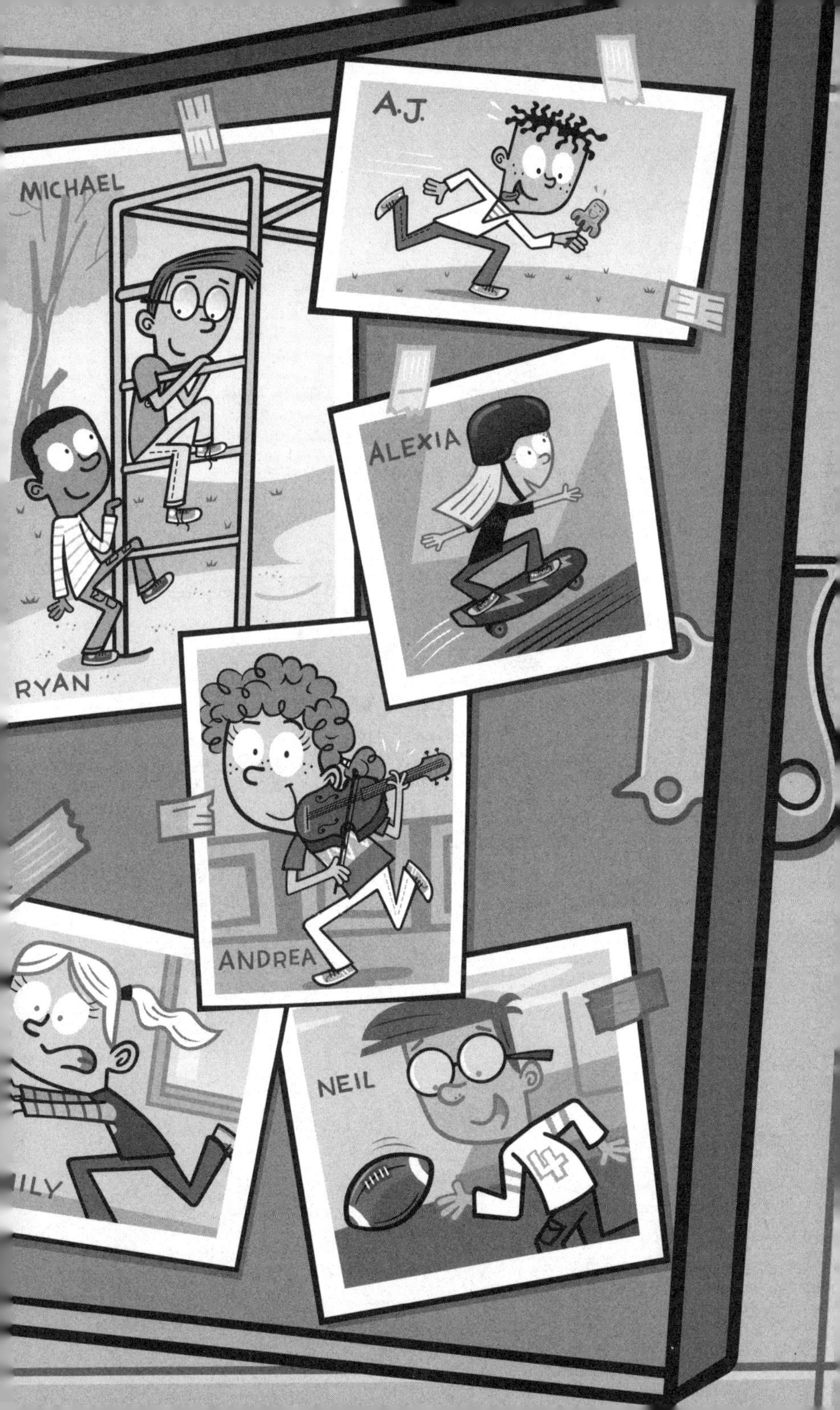

MICHAEL
RYAN
A.J.
ALEXIA
ANDREA
ILY
NEIL

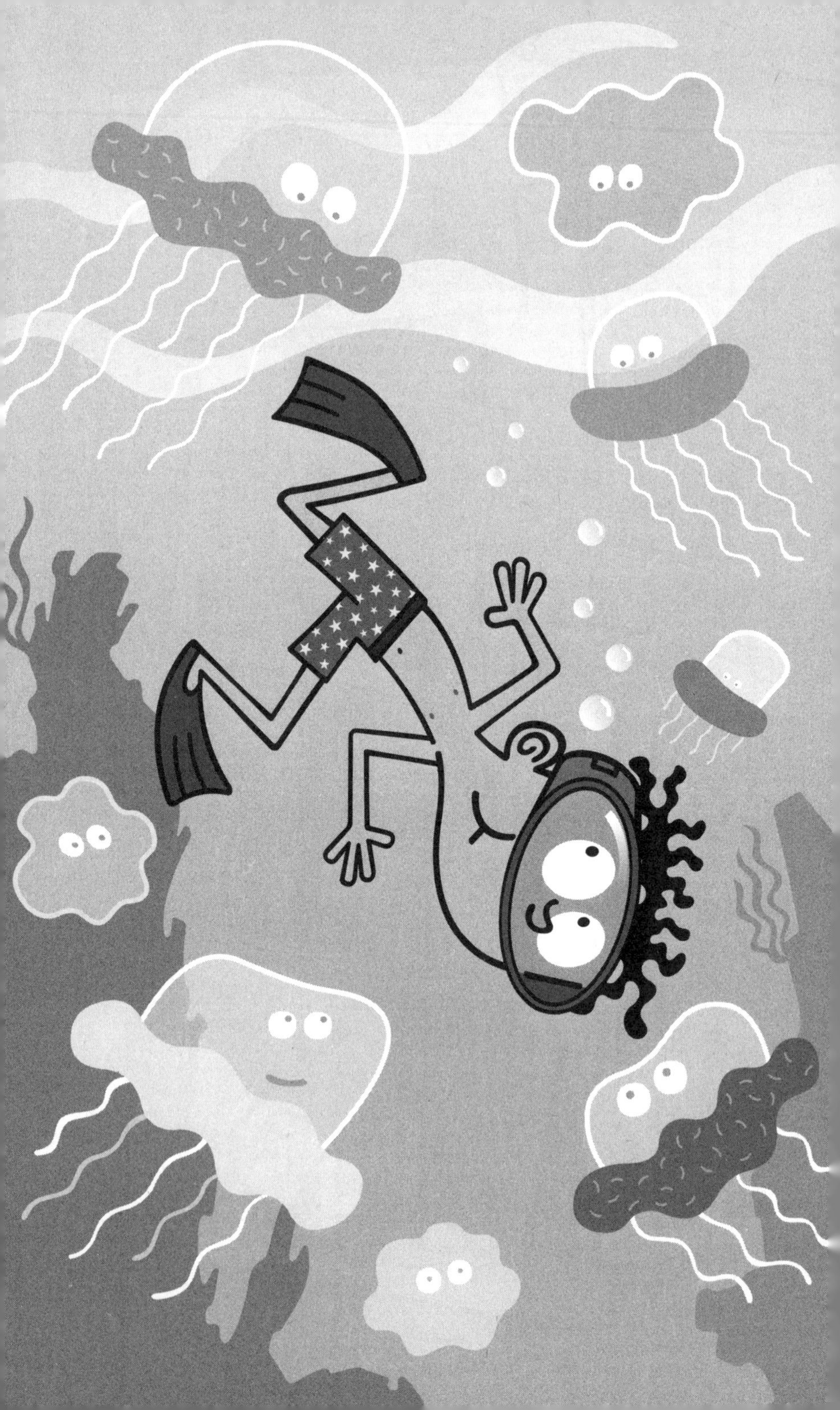

1

How Do They Get Jelly Out of Jellyfish?

My name is A.J., and I know what you're thinking. You're thinking about jellyfish. I know because that's what I'm thinking about. Jellyfish are cool. What I want to know is, if there are jellyfish in the ocean, are there also peanut butter fish? That would make sense. Because peanut butter and jelly go together really well.

My point is, we were in Miss Banks's class learning about social studies, or something like that. I'm not sure because I wasn't paying attention. Suddenly, Miss Banks called on me.

"Are you paying attention, A.J.?" she asked.

I decided to be honest because my parents always say honesty is the best policy.

"Uh . . . no."

"Were you daydreaming again?" Miss Banks asked.

"Uh . . . yeah."

"What were you thinking about, A.J.?" she asked.

"Jellyfish," I replied.

Everybody laughed even though I didn't say anything funny.

"What *about* jellyfish, A.J.?" said Miss Banks.

"If there are jellyfish in the ocean," I said, "are there also peanut butter fish?"

Everybody laughed again.

"And I was wondering how they squeeze the jelly out of jellyfish," I continued.

"I don't think jelly comes from jellyfish," Miss Banks replied.

"Then why do they call them jellyfish?" I asked.

"Jelly comes from *gelatin*, Arlo!" said Andrea Young, this annoying girl who sits next to me with curly brown hair.* She calls me by my real name because she knows I don't like it.

Andrea thinks she is *sooooo* smart

---

*Well, she has curly brown hair no matter where she sits.

because she's a member of PAC—the Principal's Advisory Committee—a group of nerds who get to boss around the principal all the time.

Andrea rolled her eyes at me, like always. I wish her eyes would roll right out of her head. I was going to say something mean to her, but I couldn't think of anything fast enough. So I just said how much I like peanut butter and jelly sandwiches.

"You probably don't even know how to *make* a peanut butter and jelly sandwich," Andrea told me.

"Why would I?" I replied. "My mom makes lunch for me."

"My mom does too," said Ryan.

"My dad makes my lunch," said Michael.

"Wait a minute," said Miss Banks. "Are you serious? You kids *really* don't know how to make a peanut butter and jelly sandwich?"

"I do!" shouted Andrea. "You take two pieces of bread. Spread peanut butter on one piece. Spread jelly on the other piece. Then you put the two pieces together. It's simple!"

Andrea smiled the smile she smiles to let everybody know she knows something nobody else knows.

Miss Banks shook her head sadly.

"What about building things?" she asked. "Raise your hand if you've ever hammered a nail or sawed a piece of wood."

Andrea was the only one who raised her hand.

"You mean hammer a fingernail?" asked Alexia.

"What's a saw?" asked Neil.

"I saw a piece of wood," I said. "With my *eyes*!"

Everybody laughed because I said something funny.

"My dad told me that hammers and saws can be dangerous," said Ryan. "You could hurt yourself."

Miss Banks shook her head again.

"Do you kids know how to *repair*

things?" she asked.

"Like what?" asked Emily.

"Like *anything*!" said Miss Banks. "What do you do when something in your house breaks?"

"We throw it out and get a new one, of course," I said. "Duh!"

Miss Banks slapped her own forehead. She slaps her forehead a lot. I'm afraid she's going to hurt herself.

2
Meet the Phelpses

The next day was Friday. Yay! The last day of the school week. After Miss Banks took attendance, the weirdest thing in the history of the world happened. An announcement came over the loudspeaker.

Well, that's not the weird part. Announcements come over the loudspeaker all the time. The weird part was what happened *after* that.

"Please report to the all-porpoise room for a surprise assembly," announced Mrs. Patty, the school secretary.

Uh-oh, I didn't like the sound of that. Sometime surprises are good, like when your parents suddenly say let's go out for ice cream. Some surprises are bad, like when you're walking on the sidewalk and a piano falls on your head.

We marched a million hundred miles to the all-porpoise room, which really needs a new name because there are no dolphins in there. When we got to the all-porpoise room, we had to sit boy-girl-boy-girl so we wouldn't talk to anybody we liked. I had to sit between annoying Andrea and crybaby Emily. Our principal, Mrs. Stoker, was up on the stage.

"Good morning, everyone," she said. "Say, do you know what nervous carpenters do?"

"WHAT?" we shouted.

"They bite their nails!" said

Mrs. Stoker. "By the way, I just started on a seafood diet. Every time I see food, I eat it. Get it? Seafood? See food?"

Mrs. Stoker is a joker. Before she was our principal, she was a stand-up comedian.

We all laughed. You should always laugh at the principal's jokes, even if they're not funny. That's the first rule of being a kid.

"But seriously," said Mrs. Stoker, "it has come to my attention . . ."*

Uh-oh. Anytime grown-ups say something has come to their attention, you *know* you did something wrong.

". . . that kids today aren't learning some of the basic skills you're going to need when

---

*Attention must be rich, because everybody has to pay it.

you grow up, like cooking and working with tools. You think cooking means turning on a microwave. You spend hours sitting still and staring at screens, *blah blah blah...*"

She went on like that for a while.

"Well, I say it's time to put down your smartphones, tablets, and video games. There's more to life than clicking, streaming, sharing, and posting. So guess what we're going to do?"

"You're going to let us go home early?" shouted a kid in the back.

"No," said Mrs. Stoker.

"Give us recess all day?" shouted a kid in the front.

"No."

"Cancel school forever?" shouted a kid in the middle.

"No!" said Mrs. Stoker. "We're going to learn how to *do* things!"

Ugh. I don't want to do things. Doing things is boring.

"In addition to art and music," said Mrs. Stoker, "we're adding two new specials to our curriculum at Ella Mentry School—career tech education and family & consumer sciences."

"What?" asked everybody in the whole school. Even the teachers didn't know what Mrs. Stoker was talking about.

"What's *that*?" somebody shouted.

"Let me explain," said Mrs. Stoker.

"When I was a child, we called them 'shop' and 'home economics.' In shop, we learned how to build things out of wood. In home ec, we learned how to cook and sew. That's what we're going to start learning at Ella Mentry School. Doesn't it sound like fun?"

"YES!" shouted all the girls.

"NO!" shouted all the boys.

"I'd like to introduce our new teachers . . ." said Mrs. Stoker.

A man and a lady came out from behind the curtain. The man was wearing an apron and a chef's hat. The lady was wearing overalls and holding a big wrench.

"Hi, everybody!" they said, waving at us.

We clapped, because that's what you're supposed to do when people come out on the stage, even if they haven't done anything yet. Nobody knows why.

"I'm going to teach career tech education," said the lady. "But you can call it woodworking. We're going to build things with wood."

"And I'm going to teach family and consumer sciences, or FCS," said the man. "We're going to cook and sew lots of cool things."

"Welcome to Ella Mentry School," said Mrs. Stoker. "Students, put your hands together for Mr. and Mrs. Phelps!"

We all clapped again.

"They're *both* named Phelps?" I mumbled. "That's an amazing coincidence."

"They're *married,* Arlo!" said Andrea. "That's why they have the same last name."

"You mean, married to *each other*?" I asked.

"Yes!"

"We're excited to be here!" Mr. Phelps said as he put his arm around Mrs. Phelps. "And it just so happens that today is our twentieth anniversary."

"Congratulations!" said Mrs. Stoker.

Wow. They've been married for twenty years? That's almost a hundred.

That's when the most awful, disgusting thing in the history of the world happened. Mrs. Phelps gave Mr. Phelps a kiss! On the *lips*!

Gross! I had to cover my eyes so I wouldn't have to witness the horrible sight.

"That's so sweet!" said Andrea. "They've

been married for twenty years, and they're still in love! Isn't that romantic?"

Ugh. Andrea said the L word. I thought I was gonna throw up.

3
Dad Puts Me to Sleep

The fourth grade was scheduled to see Mrs. Phelps on Mondays and Wednesdays and Mr. Phelps on Tuesdays and Thursdays. Four days of torture in a row! Let me tell you something right now: This story is *not* going to have a happy ending. No way.

It was hard for me to fall asleep that night. I kept thinking about sewing and cooking and having to make stuff out of wood. I was tossing and turning when my dad walked past my bedroom door.

"Are you okay, A.J.?" he asked.

"I can't sleep," I told him.

"Do you want to talk about it?" he asked. My dad is really good at helping me fall asleep.*

"Mrs. Stoker is gonna make us cook and sew and build things at school," I told him. "I don't want to do that stuff. She's mean."

"Yes, she sent an email about it to the parents," Dad replied. "What do you wish

---
*Because he's boring.

you could do instead?"

"I wish we could play video games at school," I said. "That would be cool."

"I'm sure it would," Dad replied. "But Mrs. Stoker believes it's important for kids to learn how to do things with your hands. And I think she's right."

"I play video games with my hands," I replied.

"True," Dad said, "but you and your classmates need to learn life skills that you'll be able to use when you get older."

"Playing video games is a life skill," I replied.

"Son..."

Oh no. He called me "son." Whenever

my dad calls me "son," I know he's about to launch into one of his lectures about the good old days a million hundred years ago when he was a kid.

"A.J.," he began, "when I was a kid, I used to love taking things apart. The toaster. A lamp. Our lawn mower. I learned how they worked, and I learned how to fix them when they broke. I learned how to cook for myself too. I learned how to darn my socks when they got holes in them. One time, I took apart our toilet—"

"Wait," I said. "You took apart a toilet?" That was just weird.

"Yes!" he said. "So I could understand how it worked. And when I got a new bike, I learned how to adjust the brakes, the gears..."

And he was off to the races.

"These days," my dad continued, "kids don't learn how to do these things. It's the parents' fault, I think. We created a generation of kids who can't do anything with their hands except play video games. You're used to instant gratification and getting trophies just for participating and *blah blah blah...*"

I had no idea what he was talking about, but I must admit it was relaxing to listen to the sound of his voice.

"Nowadays," Dad continued, "kids just think that everything comes from a store, or from the Internet *blah blah blah*. Darn a sock? Kids never wear socks long enough to get a hole in them *blah blah blah* sitting around for hours starting at screens *blah blah blah* eating junk food *blah blah blah* you should learn how to make healthy meals *blah blah blah...*"

Okay, I get it. Everything was better in the good old days.

"... figuring out why something doesn't work and learning how to fix it is a critical thinking skill *blah blah blah* kids learn from physical work just like they do from mental work *blah blah blah*..."

He kept talking. My mind was wandering. I was thinking about jellyfish again.

"... *blah blah blah* learn how to plan a project and build it *blah blah blah* group activity *blah blah blah* work as a team *blah blah blah*..."

When is he going to wrap it up? What a snoozefest.

"... *blah blah blah* rewards patience *blah*

blah blah . . . learn how to use tools and real-world materials *blah blah blah* . . ."

I was feeling sleepy.

". . . *blah blah blah* most of all, you'll get the thrill of creating something you made with your own hands *blah blah blah* . . ."

I couldn't keep my eyes open.

". . . *blah blah blah* and it will give you something to take home and show Mom and me. We'll be so proud of you *blah blah blah blah blah blah blah blah* . . ."

Zzzzzzzzzzzzzzzzzzzzzzzzz.

4
Measure Twice, Cut Once

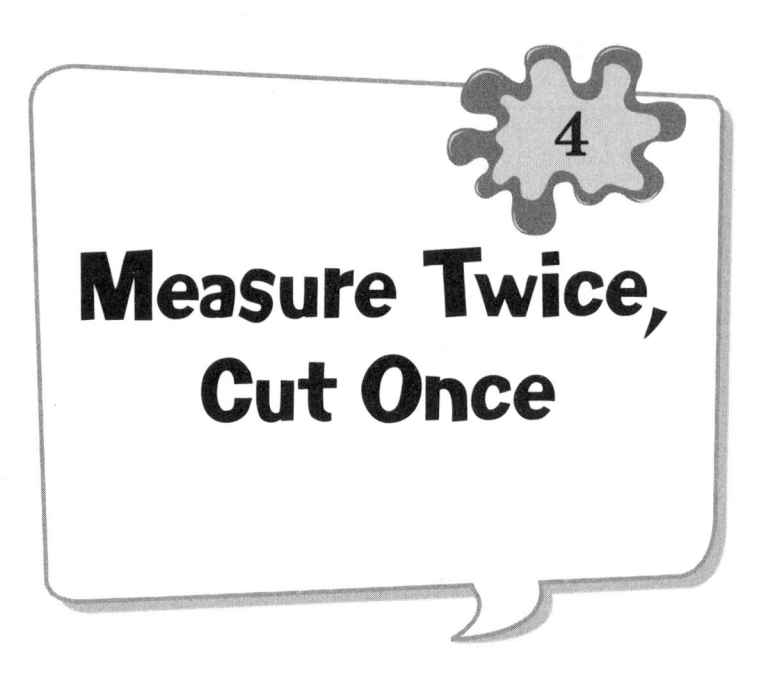

It was Monday. We walked a million hundred miles to the new woodworking room. Mrs. Phelps was waiting for us in the doorway.

There were hammers and saws and lots of other weird tools hanging all over the walls. It looked like a hardware store, or an ancient torture chamber.

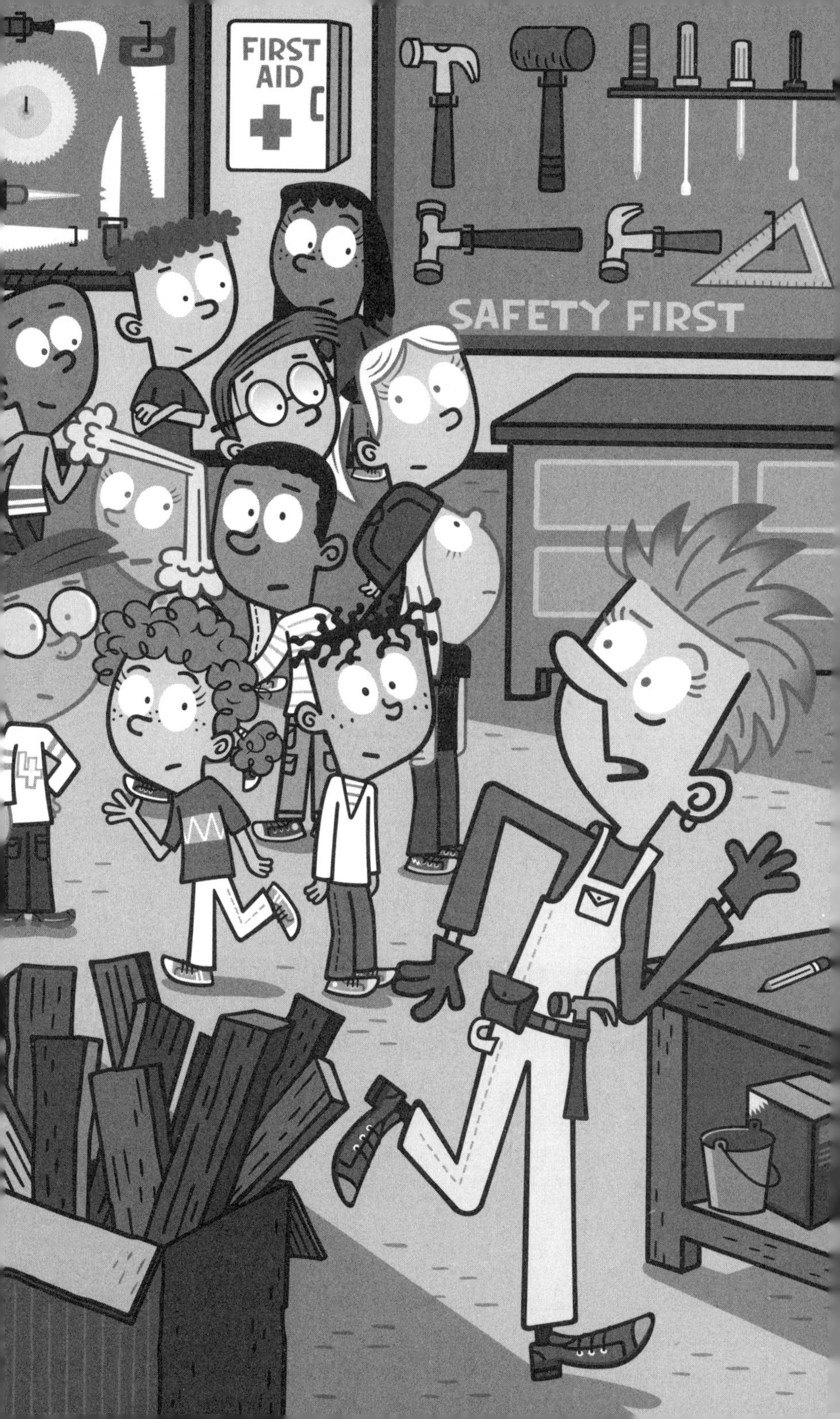
FIRST AID
SAFETY FIRST

"This room is scary," said Emily, who's scared of everything.

"That's right!" said Mrs. Phelps. "You *should* be scared! Being scared just might save your life in here."

"What are we going to build?" asked Ryan.

"Before we build *anything*," said Mrs. Phelps, "we need to talk about safety."

"Yeah, I guess you could get a nasty cut in here," said Alexia, "with all these sharp tools."

"A cut?" Mrs. Phelps snorted. "That would be the *least* of your problems. "You could cut off a *finger*! You could poke an *eye* out! You could set yourself on fire!

You could get stabbed with a screwdriver! You could saw off your *leg*!"

A few kids were whimpering.

"You could get *electrocuted* by power tools!" continued Mrs. Phelps. "You could drop an anvil on your toe! You could get your head caught in a vise! There could be an earthquake and the whole building could collapse!"

She went on and on about all the horrible things that might happen in the woodworking room. I was afraid to touch anything.

"These things happen all the time," continued Mrs. Phelps. "Vincent van Gogh cut off his ear."

"I don't think that happened while he was doing woodworking," said Andrea.

"My point is," said Mrs. Phelps, "working with wood is *dangerous*."

"Okay, we get it," said Michael. "Can we build something now?"

"We're going to start by sawing a wooden board in half," said Mrs. Phelps.

She gave each of us a board, a handsaw, a ruler, and a pencil. Then she told us all the boards were thirty inches long, and we should saw ours in half.

"Remember," said Mrs. Phelps. "Measure *twice*, cut *once*. And be careful not to saw your finger off."

Half of thirty inches is fifteen inches.* I measured my board and cut it in half.

Well, I *thought* I cut it in half. One of my halves turned out to be longer than the other half. So I measured the two halves. Oh no! One was sixteen inches and the other one was fourteen inches. I looked around. Everybody else's halves were the same size.

"Something went wrong," I said.

"Did you measure twice, like I told you to?" asked Mrs. Phelps.

"Sure," I replied. "I measured before I cut the board, and then I measured again *after* I cut the board. That's twice."

---

*I'm pretty good in math, huh?

"Arlo," said Andrea, rolling her eyes, "you're supposed to measure twice *before* you cut the board!"

"She didn't tell us that!" I complained.

Mrs. Phelps sighed and shook her head sadly.

"You need to get the board stretcher," she told me. "I loaned it to Ms. Hannah. Go to the art room and ask her for it."

Board stretcher? I never heard of a board stretcher. But I figured that Mrs. Phelps must know what she's talking about. I walked a million hundred miles to the art room.

"Hi, Ms. Hannah," I said. "Mrs. Phelps asked me to get the board stretcher from you. Do you have it?"

"Oh, I loaned it to Mr. Docker," said Ms. Hannah. "Go to the science room and get it."

I walked a million hundred miles to the science room.

"Hi, Mr. Docker," I said. "Do you have the board stretcher? Mrs. Phelps needs it back."

"I loaned it to Mrs. Yonkers," said Mr. Docker. "It must be in the computer lab."

I walked a million hundred miles to the computer lab.

"Hi, Mrs. Yonkers," I said. "Do you have the board stretcher?"

"I returned it to Mrs. Phelps," she replied.

I walked a million hundred miles back to the woodworking room.

"Nobody has the board stretcher," I told Mrs. Phelps."

"Well, that doesn't surprise me," she replied.

"Why not?"

"BECAUSE THERE'S NO SUCH THING AS A BOARD STRETCHER!" shouted Mrs. Phelps.

"What?!" I replied. "Then why did you

send me all over the school looking for it?"

"Maybe *next* time you'll remember to measure *twice* and cut *once*!" said Mrs. Phelps.

Brrrrrriiiiiiinnnnngggg! The period was over.

The bells in our school go *Brrrrrriiiiiiinnnnngggg!* Nobody knows why.

"See you on Wednesday," said Mrs. Phelps. "Next time, we're going to build birdhouses."

Birdhouses? I thought birds built their *own* houses. Isn't that what a nest is?

Mrs. Phelps is weird.

Snickerdoodles

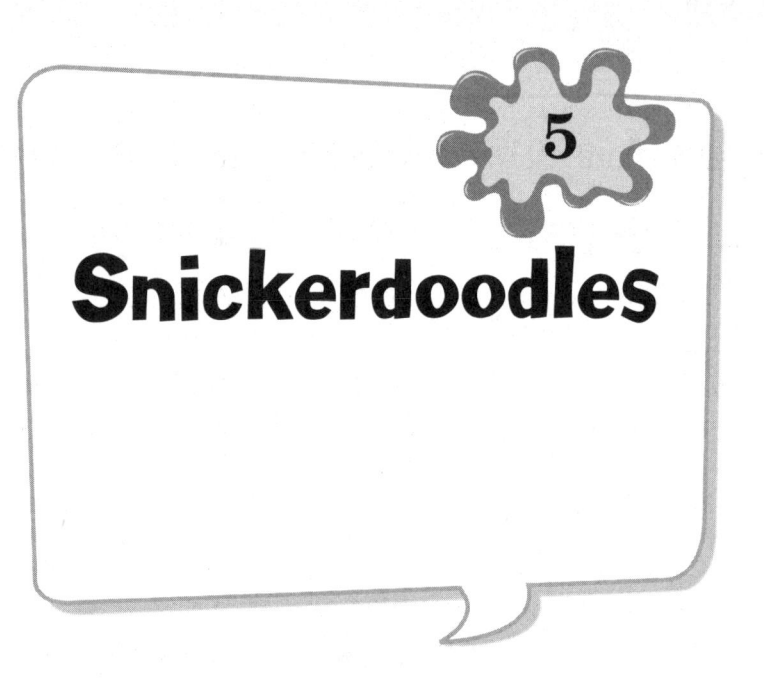

5

It was Tuesday, so we walked a million hundred miles to the new FCS room. Mr. Phelps was waiting for us in the doorway. There were pots and pans and all kinds of weird food tools all over the room. It looked like somebody's kitchen.

"Welcome to family and consumer

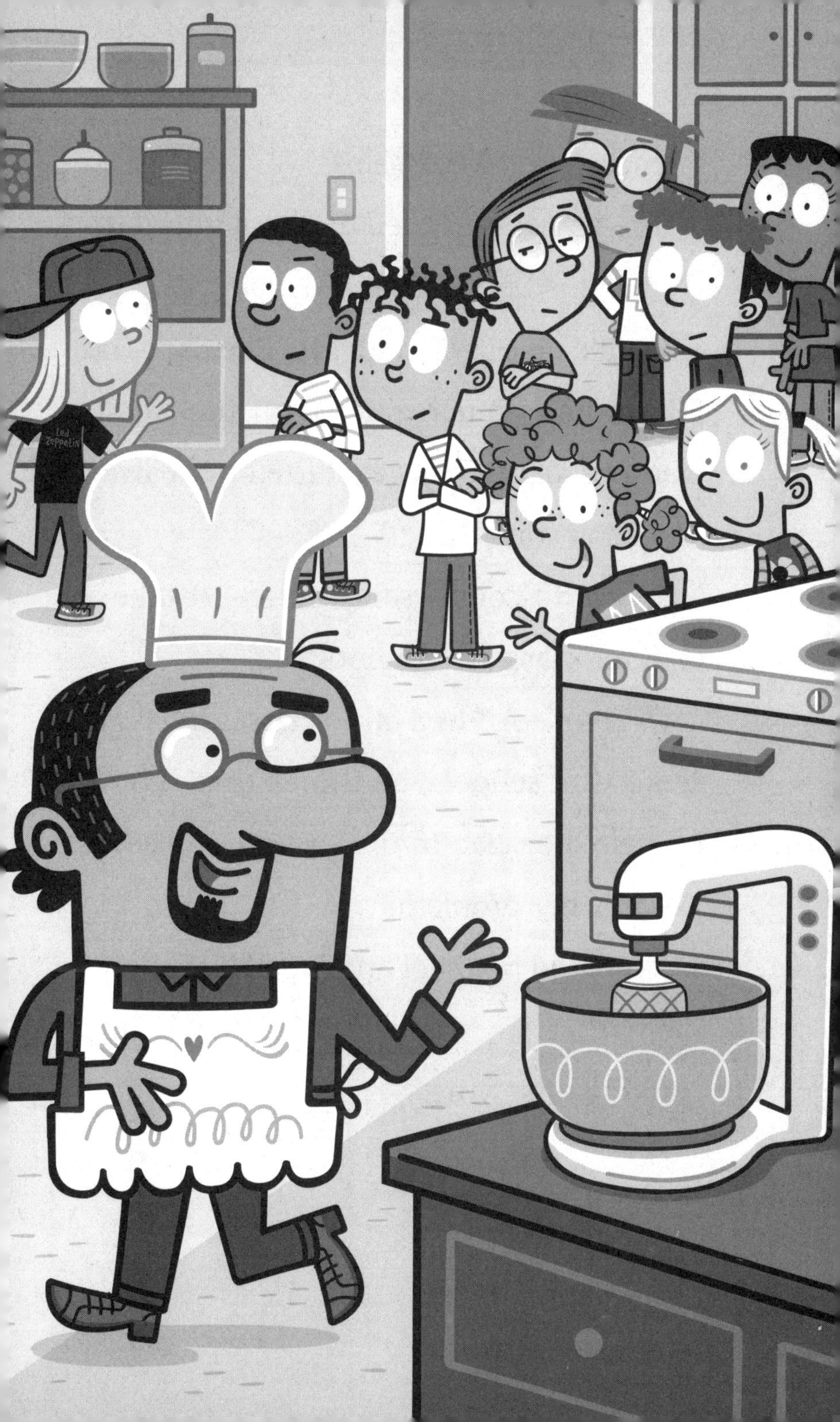
Led Zeppelin

sciences," said Mr. Phelps.

"Are you going to tell us about how dangerous it is here?" asked Alexia.

"Don't be silly," said Mr. Phelps. "The FCS room is much safer than the woodworking room. Let's get started right away and cook something!"

"I love to cook!" said Andrea. "I take a cooking class after school."

Of *course*. Andrea takes classes in *everything* after school. She thinks that's going to help her get into Harvard someday. What is her problem?

Ryan and Michael and I made an agreement that we weren't going to do any cooking or sewing.

"We don't want to cook," the three of us said, crossing our arms in front of us. If you don't want to do something, you should always cross your arms in front of you. That's the first rule of being a kid.

"Okay," said Mr. Phelps. "But if you don't help with the cooking, you can't help with the eating."

"We're not hungry," Michael said.

"Good," said Mr. Phelps. "That means there will be more snickerdoodles for the rest of us."

"Snickerdoodles!?" I shouted. "I *love* snickerdoodles!"

"Me too!" said Ryan, who will eat anything, even stuff that isn't food.

Snickerdoodles are yummy cookies that taste like cinnamon.

"Okay, we'll help cook," I said.

"Great," said Mr. Phelps. "You can start by preheating the oven to three hundred fifty degrees."

I went over and turned on the oven.

Mr. Phelps had us mix flour, sugar, baking soda, and eggs in a bowl. Cracking eggs is fun. Some of the eggshells fell into the bowl, but Mr. Phelps said it was okay because the cookies would be crunchier.

Then we divided the dough into small pieces and shaped them into little balls. Then we rolled the balls in cinnamon sugar and put them on a cookie sheet.

We had to put the balls two inches apart, because they flatten and get bigger as they cook. Finally, we put the cookie sheet in the oven.

"Mmmmm," Emily said a few minutes later. "I smell the snickerdoodles already."

That's when the weirdest thing in the history of the world happened.

Brrrrrriiiiiiinnnnngggg!

"Nobody told me there was going to be a fire drill today," said Mr. Phelps. "Okay, everybody line up in single file. We'd better turn off the oven."

He went to turn it off.

"The oven is set on five hundred fifty degrees!" Mr. Phelps shouted. "It was supposed to be three hundred fifty degrees."

Everybody looked at me.

"The five looked like a three!" I explained.

Mr. Phelps opened the oven door and looked inside.

"It's not a fire drill!" he shouted as smoke poured out of the oven. "It's a FIRE!"

"EEEEEEEK!" shouted Emily. "We're all going to die!"

"Run for your lives!" shouted Neil.

"You burned the snickerdoodles, Arlo!" shouted Andrea. "Now they're ruined!"

I wanted to run away to Antarctica and go live with the penguins. Penguins don't have to preheat ovens.

"Call 9-1-1!" shouted Ryan.

But nobody had to call 9-1-1. We could already hear the siren of a fire engine coming down the street. And you'll never believe who ran into the door a few minutes later.

Nobody! Why would you run into a door? You could break your nose. But you'll never believe who ran into the door*way*.

It was Mrs. Meyer from the fire department! You can read about her in a book called *Mrs. Meyer Is on Fire!* She was carrying a fire extinguisher, and she sprayed some white stuff inside the oven to put out the fire.

"Hooray for Mrs. Meyer!" we all shouted.

That's when Mrs. Phelps came running into the room.

"Is everybody okay?" she asked. "What's going on?"

"A.J. set the snickerdoodles on fire," said Andrea.

"I did not!"

"Did too!"

"Well, honey," said Mrs. Phelps, "I guess my woodworking room is actually safer than your cooking room."

"Very funny, Mrs. Phelps," said Mr. Phelps.*

"Oh, look," said Andrea. "Mr. and Mrs. Phelps are teasing each other! Isn't that adorable? They're in *love*!"

---

*They call each other Mr. and Mrs. Phelps? That's weird.

Ugh. She said the L word again.

Mrs. Meyer told us to go outside while the fire department checked for gas leaks. So we had to stand out on the playground for a million hundred minutes until it was safe to go back into the school. Finally, we went back to the FCS room.

"Can we make another batch of snickerdoodles?" asked Ryan.

Brrrrrriiiiiiinnnnngggg!

"Sorry," said Mr. Phelps. "It looks like we've run out of time."

Bummer in the summer!

"Don't worry," said Mr. Phelps. "We're going to bake lots of yummy things in here. Next time, we'll knead bread."

"I can bring in some bread if you need it," I said.

"No, I mean we'll *knead* bread," said Mr. Phelps.

"We have extra bread at home," said Neil. "My parents have lots of it."

"You don't understand," said Mr. Phelps. "*Knead* bread."

"Do you need anything besides bread?" asked Alexia. "I could pick something up on the way to school."

"KNEAD!" shouted Mr. Phelps. "We'll *knead* bread. Knead with a *K*."

"We're gonna put bread on our knees?" I asked.

"I don't get it," said Michael.

"Yeah," said Neil. "Why do you need bread so badly?"

"Forget it!" shouted Mr. Phelps. "See you on Thursday."

Sheesh! What's the big deal about bread? Mr. Phelps is weird.

Racecar Backward

It was Wednesday, so we walked a million hundred miles to the woodworking room.

"Do we *have* to make birdhouses?" Michael asked right away. "Can't we make swords instead?"

"No," replied Mrs. Phelps. "Swords are not appropriate for children. But I came up with a different project you might like."

She took some small blocks of wood out of the closet and gave one to each of us.

"We're making blocks of wood?" I asked.

"Oh, it's a block of wood *now*," said Mrs. Phelps. "But we're going to turn it into a racecar!"

"We're building racing cars?" Ryan said. "Cool!"

Mrs. Phelps passed out safety goggles, gloves, handsaws, and sandpaper.

"Did you know that *racecar* is a palindrome?" asked Andrea.

"What's a palindrome?" asked Neil.

"A palindrome," explained Miss Know-It-All, "is a word that's spelled the same way backward and forward."

Andrea was right, like always. Racecar is spelled r-a-c-e-c-a-r whether you spell it forward, r-a-c-e-c-a-r, or backward, r-a-c-e-c-a-r.

I hate when Andrea is right. She smiled the smile she smiles to let everybody know she knows something nobody else knows.

Mrs. Phelps showed us how to cut our wood into a wedge shape like a car. Then we sanded the wood with sandpaper to make it as smooth as possible. Then we added little weights to the body of our cars and attached the wheels. Finally, we painted our cars and glued on stickers and racing stripes. My racecar looked really cool.

"Okay, it's time to race!" said Mrs. Phelps.

She set up a big ramp she had built that used gravity to move the cars down a track. We all got to race our cars on the track two times. Mrs. Phelps used a stopwatch to record the times. Andrea's car was the fastest, *of course.*

"Now let's see if Andrea's car can beat *my* car," Mrs. Phelps said as she took a really cool-looking racecar out of her desk. It was yellow, with orange flames painted on it.*

That's when an announcement came over the loudspeaker.

---

*The car, that is. Not the desk.

"Mrs. Phelps, please report to the office."

"Excuse me," said Mrs. Phelps. And you'll never believe who walked into the door a few seconds after she left.

Nobody! Why would a person walk into a door? We went over that in Chapter Five.

But you'll never believe who walked into the door*way*.

It was Mr. Phelps!

"*Shhhhhh!*" he whispered, smiling. He picked up Mrs. Phelps's racecar and loosened one of its wheels. "Don't tell Mrs. Phelps."

Then he hurried out of the room.

"Oh, look," Andrea said, "Mr. and Mrs. Phelps play little tricks on each other! Isn't that adorable? They're in *love*!"

Ugh. She keeps saying the L word.

Mrs. Phelps came back a minute later. It turned out that she wasn't needed in the office after all. Mr. Phelps must have called the office to get his wife out of the room.

"Okay!" Mrs. Phelps said. "Now let's see if my car is faster than Andrea's."

She put her racecar on the top of the track.

She let it go.

It started rolling down the track.

One of the wheels fell off.

The car skidded off the track and

crashed into the floor.

"Who loosened a wheel on my car?" Mrs. Phelps shouted angrily.

I looked at Andrea. Andrea looked at Michael. Michael looked at Alexia. Alexia looked at Neil. Neil looked at Ryan. Ryan looked at Emily. We were all looking at each other.

Brrrrrriiiiiiinnnnngggg! Woodworking was over.

"It was Mr. Phelps," I said. Because honesty is the best policy.

Baking Baguettes

7

It was Thursday, so we walked a million hundred miles to the FCS room.

"It's time to knead the bread!" said Mr. Phelps.

Guess what? It turns out that *kneading* bread and *needing* bread are not the same thing! Who knew? They should really have different-sounding words for those things. It would make life a lot easier.

Anyway, we had to knead the bread so we could bake baguettes. A baguette is a yummy kind of bread with crispy crust and chewy insides. The coolest part is that baguettes are really long and skinny. Mr. Phelps told us that a few years back, some people made a baguette that was over four hundred feet long!

"WOW!" we said, which is also "WOW" backward.

There are just four ingredients in a baguette—flour, water, salt, and yeast. We mixed them together and shaped the dough into four baguette shapes. The dough was really soft and sticky. Our baguettes were so long, they barely fit into the oven.

While the baguettes were baking, Mr. Phelps said we had some time before the period was over.

"Let's make a Jell-O mold!" he said.

"Yuck!" I replied. "I don't want to eat mold. Mold can make you sick."

Andrea rolled her eyes.

"You don't eat mold, dumbhead!" she told me. "You put the Jell-O into a mold that's made of metal."

They should really have two different words for "mold." It would make life a lot easier.

I was going to say something mean to Little Miss Perfect, but we had to make the Jell-O. Mr. Phelps helped us pour red Jell-O powder into a bowl and add boiling water. We stirred it with a spoon until the powder was dissolved, then we added some cold water. Then we poured the Jell-O into a big mold that was in the shape of a flower.

"Does anybody have any questions?" asked Mr. Phelps.

I raised my hand.

"Is Jell-O made from jellyfish?" I asked.

Andrea rolled her eyes.

"No, I don't believe so," said Mr. Phelps.

"Then why is it called Jell-O?" I asked.

"I really don't know," said Mr. Phelps.

"What *do* they make out of jellyfish?" I asked.

"I have no idea."*

---

*Boy, for a cooking teacher, he doesn't know much.

It was time to put our Jell-O mold into the refrigerator. That's when an announcement came over the loudspeaker.

"Mr. Phelps, please report to the office."

"I'll be right back," he said as he left the room. And you'll never believe who walked through the door a few seconds later.

Nobody! Are you even paying attention? YOU CAN'T WALK THROUGH A DOOR! But you'll never believe who walked through the door*way*.

It was Mrs. Phelps!

"Shhhhhh!" she whispered, smiling mischievously. Mrs. Phelps took a bottle of vegetable oil from a cabinet and dribbled

a bunch of it on the floor near the refrigerator.

"Be careful," she said as she hurried out of the room. "And don't tell Mr. Phelps."

"Why did she do that?" asked Emily.

"Who knows?" I said. "She's weird."

"That wasn't a very nice thing to do," said Andrea. "It could be dangerous to have oil on the floor."

A minute later, Mr. Phelps came back. He told us he wasn't needed in the office after all.

"The bell is about to ring," he said. "I'll put the Jell-O mold into the fridge and bring it to your classroom after it is solid."

He picked up the Jell-O mold and brought it to the fridge. But just before he was about to open the door, his foot slipped.

"Whoa!" Mr. Phelps shouted, and then he went flying.

He landed on his back, and the Jell-O

mold landed on Emily's desk. Liquid red Jell-O was all over the floor and all over Mr. Phelps.

"Who put oil on the floor?" he asked as we helped him up.

I looked at Emily. Emily looked at Ryan. Ryan looked at Neil. Neil looked at Alexia.

Alexia looked at Andrea. Andrea looked at Michael. We were all looking at each other.

"It was Mrs. Phelps," I said. Because honesty is the best policy.

Brrrrrriiiiiiinnnnngggg!

That's when the weirdest thing in the history of the world happened. Mr. Phelps started crying.

8
Crying

It's weird when grown-ups cry in front of you. They're not supposed to cry.

"What's the matter?" we all said as we gathered around Mr. Phelps.

"Mrs. Phelps hates me," he said, wiping his eyes.

"She doesn't hate you," we assured him.

"You've been married for twenty years," said Andrea. "You love each other."

Ugh. The L word again.

"Then why is she always saying mean things to me?" sniffled Mr. Phelps. "Why is she always *doing* mean things to me?"

It *was* pretty mean to put oil on the floor to make Mr. Phelps slip and spill the Jell-O. But it was also mean for him to loosen the wheel on Mrs. Phelps's racecar.

"You've done mean things to her too," Alexia pointed out.

"She started it," said Mr. Phelps.

We had to go back to class, so we couldn't stay with Mr. Phelps any longer. Before we left, we kept telling him that his wife didn't hate him, but I don't know if he believed us.

"Don't tell Mrs. Phelps that she made me cry," he begged us before we left.

The next day was Friday, so there was no woodworking or FCS. We were on the playground during recess, swinging on the swings.

What do you think Mr. and Mrs. Phelps are doing on their day off?" asked Alexia.

"They're probably at home arguing with each other," said Ryan. "They don't seem to like each other very much."

"I think Mr. and Mrs. Phelps have marriage problems," said Andrea.

"Wait a minute," I said to Andrea. "Aren't *you* the one who's always saying they tease each other and play tricks on each other because they love each other?"*

"Well, I changed my mind, okay?" replied Andrea. "My mother is a psychologist. She taught me a lot. Now I see that the Phelpses have an unhealthy relationship."

---
*I can't believe I said the L word out loud.

"Do you think they're gonna get divorced?" asked Ryan.

"I don't know."

"We should *do* something," said Emily.

"It's none of our business," said Michael.

"But maybe we can help save their marriage," said Neil.

"What can *we* do?" asked Alexia. "We're just kids."

Brrrrrriiiiiiinnnnngggg!

Recess was over. As we walked a million hundred miles back to class, we passed the woodworking room. The door was open. And you'll never believe who was in there.

I'm not gonna tell you.

Okay, okay, I'll tell you.

It was Mrs. Phelps! Her eyes were red, and it looked like she had been crying.

"Mrs. Phelps!" said Emily. "What are you doing here? Isn't this your day off?"

"Mr. Phelps and I are fighting," she said, wiping her eyes with a tissue. "I wanted to go somewhere I could be alone."

"What's wrong?" we all said as we gathered around Mrs. Phelps.

"Mr. Phelps hates me," she said, wiping her eyes some more and whimpering.

"He doesn't hate you," we assured her.

"You've been married for twenty years," said Emily. "He loves you."

"Then why is he always saying mean things to me?" asked Mrs. Phelps. "Why is he always *doing* mean things to me?"

"Sometimes you do mean things to him too," said Alexia.

"Well, he started it," said Mrs. Phelps.

We had to get back to class, so we couldn't stay with Mrs. Phelps. We told her that Mr. Phelps doesn't hate her, but I don't think she believed us.

"Don't tell Mr. Phelps that he made me cry," she begged before we left.

The Last Straw

9

As the weeks went on, we had a great time learning how to cook and sew and build stuff.

In woodworking with Mrs. Phelps, we made chessboards, spice racks, step stools, clothespin stands, pencil holders, cutting boards, and wooden boats. Alexia even built her own guitar at home and brought it in for show-and-tell. It was cool.

In FCS with Mr. Phelps, we made doughnuts, marshmallows, pretzels, cinnamon toast, pizza, macaroni and cheese, and Rice Krispies treats. We even made scrambled eggs in a plastic bag. That was weird.

We learned how to thread a needle and sew on a button. We made aprons, beanbags, stuffed animals, and pillows in the shape of our initials. Andrea made a scrunchie, whatever that is.

And of course, we made baguettes every week, because they're *soooooo* yummy.

We were getting really good at cooking and sewing and building stuff. Mrs. Stoker was happy that we were learning real life skills instead of staring at screens.

Mr. and Mrs. Phelps are both great teachers, and we really liked them.

The only problem was that the Phelpses just couldn't seem to get along with each other. Mrs. Phelps would do or say something mean to Mr. Phelps, and then he would do or say something mean to her. We would see them arguing in the hallway with angry faces, and then one of them would storm off in a huff. They never held hands anymore. They barely spoke. The situation seemed to be getting worse.

Then came the last Wednesday in March, when the weirdest thing in the history of the world happened. We came to woodworking class, and Mrs. Phelps said our project for the day was to build a trunk—a big box to store blankets and stuff. She had the wood planks and all the tools ready for us. We spent most of the period measuring and sawing and sanding and hammering. It was a team effort.

The trunk was really big. It was so deep that none of us could reach the bottom to finish sandpapering it. So Mrs. Phelps took out her cell phone and texted Mr. Phelps. She asked him to come to the woodworking room to help. He showed up a minute later.

And here's the weird part—while Mr. Phelps was leaning over the trunk with the sandpaper, Mrs. Phelps lifted up her leg and gave him a big shove with her boot!

He fell into the trunk! Mrs. Phelps quickly closed the lid and locked it.

"That oughta hold him for a while," she said, chuckling.

"Help! Help!" shouted Mr. Phelps. "Let me out!"

That was weird.

* * *

I guess Mr. Phelps eventually got out of the trunk, because the next morning he was there when we walked into the FCS room.

"What are we going to make today, Mr. Phelps?" I asked.

"Tomorrow is Mrs. Phelps's birthday," he replied. "So we're going to bake her a cake."

"YAY!" we all shouted, which is also "YAY" backward.

"Oh, good," Andrea whispered. "Maybe they stopped fighting."

Mr. Phelps helped us mix the flour with water, eggs, and butter. Then he gave us a big measuring cup full of sugar to pour in.

"That's a lot of sugar!" said Andrea. "Are you sure it's not too much?"

"I want the cake to be extra sweet," Mr. Phelps explained.

We put the cake in the oven to bake. When it was ready, we decorated it with chocolate icing and stuck candles into the top.

Mr. Phelps lit the candles and told us to turn out the lights. He texted for Mrs. Phelps to come to the FCS room.

"HAPPY BIRTHDAY TO YOU . . ." we all sang as she walked in the room. She looked surprised and happy.

"Can we each have a piece of cake?" I asked.

"Oh, this cake is *just* for Mrs. Phelps," Mr. Phelps said as he cut a piece. "It's *her* birthday."

Booooooooo!

Mr. Phelps put the piece of cake on a plate and handed it to Mrs. Phelps.

"Sweets for the sweet," he said.

Mrs. Phelps took a bite.

About a second later, her eyes bugged out and she wrinkled up her nose.

"Ugh!" she shouted, spitting cake all over the floor. "This cake is *horrible*! Did you put in salt instead of sugar?"

"Oops," Mr. Phelps replied. "My bad!"

"You did that on purpose!" shouted Mrs. Phelps. "That's the last straw!"

Huh? What did straws have to do with

anything?

Why are people always running out of straws? You'd think they would buy a new box of straws before they were down to the last one.*

---

*People should think ahead so they don't run out of straws all the time.

10
Choose Your Weapons

Mrs. Phelps was *really* angry about her salty birthday cake.

"I can't work at the same school with you anymore!" she shouted.

"Same here!" replied Mr. Phelps. "One of us has to leave. And it should be *you*."

"I'm not going *anywhere*!" shouted Mrs. Phelps.

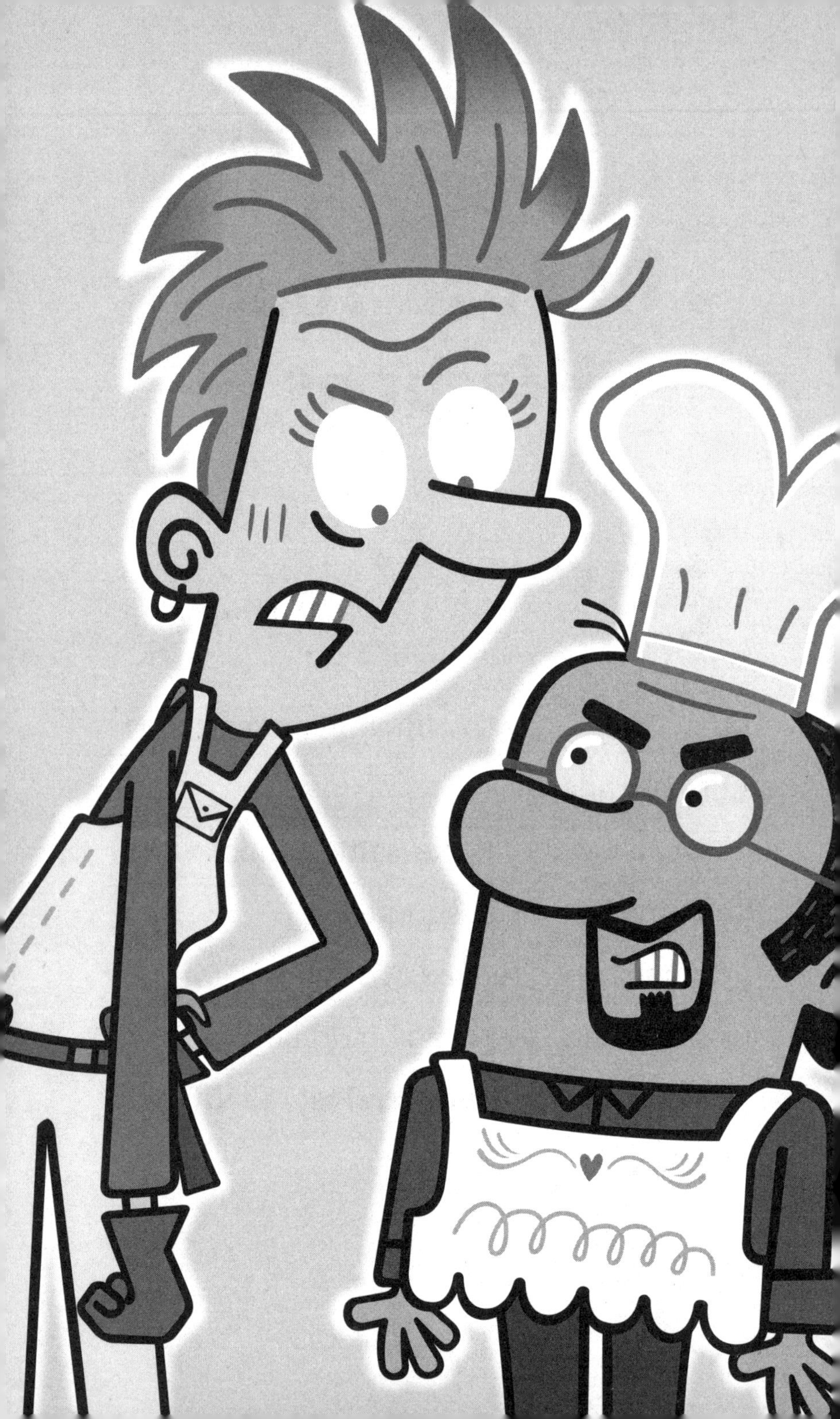

"Well, me neither!" shouted Mr. Phelps. "There's only one way to settle this. I challenge you to a duel. The loser has to leave the school."

"I accept!" said Mrs. Phelps. "Meet me on the playground, right after dismissal."

"Oh, snap!" said Ryan. "They're going to have a duel!"

"What's a duel?" Emily asked.

"Back in the old days," Ryan explained, "people who had an argument would challenge each other to a fight with weapons. It was sort of like those lightsaber fights in *Star Wars*."

"I don't approve of such violence," Andrea said.

"What do you have against violins?" I asked her.

"Not violins, Arlo!" shouted Andrea. "Violence!"

I know the difference between violins and violence. I was just yanking Andrea's chain.

Mr. and Mrs. Phelps stuck their faces right next to each other, but they weren't kissing. They were sneering.

"We need to choose our weapons," sneered Mrs. Phelps.

"Pillows," sneered Mr. Phelps.

"Nerf balls," sneered Mrs. Phelps.

"Water pistols!" sneered Mr. Phelps.

"Super Soakers!" sneered Mrs. Phelps.

There was a lot of sneering going on!

"Too bad we didn't make swords in woodworking," I said. "A duel with swords would be cool."

"How about baguettes?" suggested Ryan. "They're sort of like swords."

"YES!" shouted Mr. and Mrs. Phelps at the same time. "Baguettes it is!"

Ryan ran to the FCS room to get some of the extra baguettes we had baked. When he came back to the playground, he handed one baguette to Mr. Phelps and another one to Mrs. Phelps.

"This school isn't big

enough for the both of us," snarled Mrs. Phelps.

"That's right," Mr. Phelps snarled right back. "It's you or me. One of us will have to go."

"You're going *down!*" snarled Mrs. Phelps.

"Oh, I don't *think* so!" snarled Mr. Phelps.

There sure was a lot of snarling going on. Even Andrea was snarling—at me.

"This is all *your* fault, Arlo!" Andrea snarled.

"What?" I complained. "What did *I* do?"

"You set the snickerdoodles on fire," Andrea told me. "You told Mrs. Phelps that Mr. Phelps loosened the wheel on her racecar. Then you told Mr. Phelps that Mrs. Phelps put oil on the floor to make her spill the Jell-O."

"It's not my fault that they don't get along!" I snarled at Andrea.

"If you knew how to make a peanut butter and jelly sandwich," snarled Andrea, "Mr. and Mrs. Phelps wouldn't even *be* here in the *first* place!"

"Oh, yeah?" I said, trying to think of a comeback to Andrea. "If *you* hadn't been born, *you* wouldn't be here in the first place."*

Andrea looked sad, like she was about to cry.

"Because of *you*, Arlo," she whined, "I'll

---

*I guess I showed *her*!

never go to Harvard."

I didn't see how any of that stuff would prevent Andrea from going to Harvard.

Brrrrrriiiiiiinnnnngggg!

The dismissal bell rang. It was time for the big duel.

11

Duels Are Cool

We grabbed our backpacks and followed Mr. and Mrs. Phelps out to the playground. Just about every kid in the school came over, and we all formed a big circle around them.

Holding their baguettes in front of them, Mr. and Mrs. Phelps stood back-to-back.

"Oooh, look!" I said. "Their tushies are touching!"

"Knock it off, Arlo!" said Andrea. "This is *serious*."

Andrea was right. It *was* serious. Okay, no more jokes for the rest of the story.

Mr. and Mrs. Phelps had angry looks on their faces. They were about to duel. There was electricity in the air.

Well, not really. If there was electricity in the air, everybody would have been electrocuted. But we were all glued to our seats.

Well, not exactly. We were just standing there. It would be weird to glue yourself to a seat. How would you get the glue off your pants?

Sorry, no more jokes. The point is . . . it was *exciting*. You should have *been* there! We got to see it live and in person.

"Are you ready?" asked Mrs. Phelps.

"Ready when you are," replied Mr. Phelps.

They held up their baguettes. Then they took three steps forward.

"One . . . two . . . three . . ."

They turned around to face each other.

"May the best teacher win!" Mrs. Phelps shouted as she waved her baguette in the air. *"En garde!"*

The Phelpses circled each other for a few seconds, like tigers.

Then Mrs. Phelps hit Mr. Phelps on the

shoulder with her baguette.

Then Mr. Phelps hit Mrs. Phelps in the stomach with his baguette.

They were swinging their baguettes up and down, back and forth, just like in *Star*

Wars. That's when the weirdest thing in the history of the world happened.

Andrea shouted, "THAT'S THE LAST STRAW!"

Not straws again!

She ran out to the middle of the circle.

"STOP!" Andrea shouted as she separated Mr. and Mrs. Phelps. "STOP THE DUEL!"

"Gasp!" everybody gasped.

"What are you doing?" asked Mr. Phelps.

"Violence won't solve your problems!" shouted Andrea. "My mother is a psychologist. She told me you need to have an intervention!"

An inter-WHAT?

"What's that?" everybody asked.

"An intervention," explained Andrea, "is when a person is confronted by their friends or family and convinced they have to deal with a problem."

Andrea grabbed both baguettes out of the hands of Mr. and Mrs. Phelps. She broke them in half and tossed them on the ground.*

"NO MORE DUELING!" Andrea shouted, "One of you is going to get hurt. Violence is not the way to settle your differences."

"Yeah!" Alexia shouted as she ran into the circle. "You two have been married

---

*I guess they didn't knead them anymore.

for twenty years. You couldn't last that long if you didn't love each other. But everybody has different opinions about things. You argue. That's okay. It's possible for two people to argue and still love each other."

Honesty is the best policy, so I ran into the big circle too.

"We saw both of you crying," I told the Phelpses. "And we saw each of you saying the other one hates you."

"You were crying?" Mr. and Mrs. Phelps said to each other.

And you'll never believe who ran into the circle at that moment.

It was Mrs. Stoker, our principal! I thought she was going to start cracking jokes like she always does, but for once she didn't.

"These kids are absolutely right!" Mrs. Stoker shouted. "Look at A.J. and Andrea.

They argue all the time. But you kids really like each other, don't you?"

"Of course!" said Andrea. "I like A.J."

"And you like Andrea too," said Mrs. Stoker. "Isn't that right, A.J.?"

Everybody turned to look at me.

If I said I *didn't* like Andrea, Mr. and Mrs. Phelps might split up and get a divorce. And if I said I *did* like Andrea, it might save their marriage, but the guys would make fun of me for the rest of my life.

I didn't know what to say. I didn't know what to do. I was faced with the hardest decision of my life. I had to think fast.

"Uh . . . I guess so," I finally mumbled.

"You guess *what*, A.J.?" asked Mrs. Stoker.

"I guess I like Andrea," I said softly.

"I CAN'T HEAR YOU," said Mrs. Stoker, who probably needs to get hearing aids.

"I guess I like Andrea," I said a little louder.

There was total silence. You could have heard a pin drop.

That is, if anyone had brought a pin with them. But why would you bring a pin to the playground?

"Ooooh!" Ryan said. "A.J. finally admitted he likes Andrea. That proves it. They're in LOVE!"

"When are you gonna get married?" asked Michael.

If those guys weren't my best friends, I would hate them.

It was horrible, but I think I did the right thing by saying I like Andrea. Because after I said it, Mr. and Mrs. Phelps looked at each other.

"If A.J. and Andrea can get along," said Mr. Phelps, "I guess we can too."

"We have our differences," said Mrs. Phelps, "but we still love each other."

She took Mr. Phelps's hand and gave him a kiss.

"I love you, sweetie," said Mr. Phelps.

"I love you, too, darling," said Mrs. Phelps.

Sweetie? Darling? Ugh. Disgusting! I thought I was gonna throw up.

We watched as Mr. and Mrs. Phelps walked down the street to their car. They were holding hands the whole way.

So I guess the story had a happy ending after all. Maybe we'll make more snickerdoodles and Jell-O. Maybe we'll get some dolphins in the all-porpoise room. Maybe my dad will take apart our toilet. Maybe we'll get another box of straws. Maybe somebody will invent the board stretcher. Maybe people will stop walking into doors and saying the L word. Maybe Andrea will go to Harvard. Maybe Mr. and Mrs. Phelps will live happily ever after. Maybe I'll find out how they get jelly out of a jellyfish.

But it won't be easy!

My Weird School

My Weird School Graphic Novels

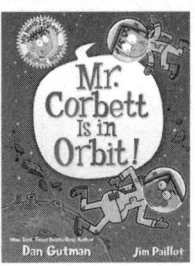

My Weirder School

My Weirdest School

My Weirder-est School

My Weirdtastic School

My Weird School Fast Facts

My Weird School Daze

HARPER
An Imprint of HarperCollinsPublishers

harpercollinschildrens.com